The Hispanic Mennonite Church
in North America
1932–1982

The Hispanic Mennonite Church in North America

1932-1982

Rafael Falcón

Translated by
Ronald Collins

HERALD PRESS
Scottdale, Pennsylvania
Kitchener, Ontario
1986

Library of Congress Cataloging-in-Publication Data

Falcón, Rafael.
  The Hispanic Mennonite Church in North America,
1932-1982.

  Translation of: La Iglesia Menonita hispaña en
Norte América, 1932-1982.
  Bibliography: p.
  Includes index.
  1. Hispanic American Mennonites—History—20th
century.   I. Title.
BX8128.H56F3413   1985   289.7'73'08968   85-30220
ISBN 0-8361-1282-2

THE HISPANIC MENNONITE CHURCH IN
NORTH AMERICA, 1932-1982
Copyright © 1986 by Herald Press, Scottdale, Pa. 15683
  Published simultaneously in Canada by Herald Press,
  Kitchener, Ont. N2G 4M5
Library of Congress Catalog Card Number: 85-30220
International Standard Book Number: 0-8361-1282-2
Printed in the United States of America
Design by Alice B. Shetler

90 89 88 87 86 85 10 9 8 7 6 5 4 3 2 1

To the pioneers of the thirties
To the movers of the forties and the fifties
To the pillars of the years of organization
To all those who have made this precious story a reality.

CONTENTS

PREFACE

This book is an English translation of *La Iglesia Menonita Hispana en Norte América: 1932–1982* by Rafael Falcón (Herald Press, 1985). As an aid to finding the histories of specific congregations, their names are given in Spanish with an English translation. Both names are given in the index even though only the Spanish name appears on the page indicated.

A considerable number of the congregations include some form of "Evangelical Mennonite" in their name. For the Hispanic congregations this is a description of their character, not a denominational affiliation. None of the Hispanic congregations in this volume are Evangelical Mennonite in the denominational sense but probably all of them would affirm that they are Evangelical Mennonites in the sense that their birth, their behavior, and their being center in the "evangel."

For the Hispanic, to be the church is to evangelize thus nothing is more natural than to call themselves "Evangelical Mennonites."

Ronald Collins
Goshen College
Goshen, Indiana

January 1985

13

INTRODUCTION

At the present time Hispanics make up the most rapidly growing minority group in North America. This phenomenal growth rate is not due merely to a high birth rate but to one of the largest mass immigrations recorded in contemporary history. These new arrivals, together with those who have been there for generations, have converted the North American continent, with its more than 20 million Spanish speakers, into the sixth largest Spanish-speaking area of the world, preceded only by Mexico, Colombia, Argentina, Spain, and Peru.

In the beginning of the twentieth century, the Mennonite Church responded to this great challenge in its own backyard: it did not have to go overseas to begin work among the Spanish population. From these first contacts has come a solid church that has just celebrated its fiftieth anniversary.

The purpose of this book is to relate the genesis and the development of this church that today is known as the Hispanic Mennonite Church of North America. In the writing of this history we have given special attention to the major branch of the denomination and the one that has done the most work among Hispanics, the Mennonite Church. Since the Mennonite Brethren and the General Conference Mennonites have also worked among Hispanics, although on a smaller scale, we have included a panorama of the history of each in the appendices.

In order to study the Hispanic Mennonite conglomerate within its historic context, it seemed convenient to present a synthesis of the beginnings of the Mennonite Church and its arrival in North America. Then we include a chapter for each of the following: the beginnings of the Hispanic Mennonite Church of North America, the years of thrust and organization, and the history of each of the congregations and their programs. This is followed by an interpretive chapter treating the growth and challenges that the group has so intensely experienced.

In addition, we include a series of appendices that supplement the preceding information. The first relates the history of the congregations that have disappeared. The following six include: the congregations in chronological order of their founding, congregational memberships from 1960 to 1981, a list of congregations by conference, the location of the congregations, and a panoramic history of the Mennonite Brethren and the General Conference Mennonites.

The celebration of the fiftieth anniversary of the Hispanic Mennonite Church, the profound desire of a genuine and correct vision of this ethnic group, together with the latent and obvious need of a total study of the theme proposed in the title of this volume are the motives that have produced this work.

I would not wish to end this brief introduction without first expressing my most profound gratitude to the persons to whom I am indebted for the realization of this work: to all the leaders and pastors for having answered with much kindness my many questions and for giving me precious information; to the students of the Hispanic Mennonite History course for their valuable papers, which served as a starting point for my work; to Judy, my dear sister, for her valuable work in the initial investigations; to my wife, Christine, for deciphering and typing the manuscript, but for more than that: for being an instrument of strength and inspiration to continue writing. For them and for all those who in one form or another gave me assistance or stimulation in the realization of this sizable undertaking, my most sincere appreciation.

Rafael Falcón
Goshen College
Goshen, Indiana

THE BACKGROUND

1
THE BACKGROUND

The followers of Jesus Christ formed the church. In the beginning it was pure, simple, obedient, and faithful, but gradually strange teachings filtered into the church, distorting, corrupting, and ignoring the Word of God. Thus, by the time of the Middle Ages the church had lost its vitality and integrity. It was thought that the church was capable of storing up good works in a treasury of merits and could exchange these for the sufferings that the dead had deserved because of their sins. The church also declared that it could guarantee pardon for the agony of purgatory, the place of suffering before going to heaven, even before committing the sin. These guarantees, known as indulgences, were sold by the church. The church taught and practiced the baptism of all infants. In addition to God, Father, Son, and Holy Spirit, prayers were directed to saints, apostles, martyrs, angels, and, especially, Mary, the blessed Virgin. It was thought that God had granted to the clergy the power of transubstantiation, that is, the belief that the host of communion is changed miraculously into the body and the blood of the Lord. Also the church, in order to satisfy every human need added many holy ceremonies to the seven sacraments.

Because of this situation a variety of writers and reformers began to call for a renewal of the church. This desire for renewal had been fed by the Renaissance interest in the study of the literature and art of ancient Greece and Rome. The scholars and intellectuals of that moment were interested in the original languages of the Bible and as they continued their study they began to doubt many of the teachings of the medieval church.

Although there were already reformers during the Middle Ages such as Peter Waldo, John Wycliffe, and John Hus, it was not until the sixteenth century that the Reformation reached its climax. During this period God raised up reformers such as Conrad Grebel, Felix Mantz, and George Blaurock. Based on the Bible these men of God preached and taught a gospel that was quite radical for their times. They baptized the adults that believed and for such acts were called Anabaptists, which means rebaptizers. Among these reformers emerged the key Anabaptist figure: Menno Simons (1496–1561).[1] His followers were called Menists first and later Mennonites, as they are still known today.

The ideal of the Mennonites, called "the left wing" of the Reformation, was to reform the Christian church according to the model of the apostles. For this reason they rejected the ecclesiastical tradition of the Roman Catholic Church. But the Mennonites went much farther than the Protestant groups of their day (Anglicans, Reformed, Lutherans) in their intent to restore the true essence of the church. In denouncing the error of infant baptism and declaring that only the believer could interpret the Scriptures, they rejected completely the church-state system. On the basis of biblical texts (such as Matthew 5:39), they desired a pacifist, antimilitaristic church that would conquer evil with good, a church of active love toward its enemies. They did not want to practice any form of violence. They desired a simple life that did not imitate the worldly values of society. They wanted to have a church that studied and followed the teachings of the Bible as a guide for their Christian life.[2]

This revolutionary action on the part of the Mennonites produced both negative and positive consequences. Many were persecuted, exiled, and killed. For these reasons many had to emigrate to other countries in search of more favorable conditions. But as they fled from their persecutors, they spread their faith to every corner they reached and left behind nuclei of Christians that professed an Anabaptist faith.

In spite of their optimistic attitude, the problems of the exiled Anabaptists continued to increase. The imprisonment and death of their leaders, together with the repression by the government and the church, helped to extinguish the evangelistic impetus that characterized them during this first stage. After this dynamic beginning they became engrossed with simply surviving as a community.

Already after the seventeenth century the European Mennonites began to emigrate to North America in search of more hospitable conditions in which to practice their faith. By 1644 there were Dutch Mennonite businessmen who knew the route to New Amsterdam (known today as New York). In 1663 a Dutchman by the name of Cornelius Plockhoy established a colony in Delaware, in which various Mennonites participated. However, it was not until 1683 that the first permanent Mennonite settlement was established in North America at Germantown, Pennsylvania. The 35 inhabitants of this colony came from Germany on October 6, 1683, having been invited by William Penn, the founder of the Pennsylvania colony. Although the original Mennonites of Germantown were from Germany, those who came after 1707 were from Switzerland. The Mennonites brought their German dialect with them to Pennsylvania and soon became known as the "Pennsylvania Dutch."

There have been four principle immigrations of Mennonites to North America. The immigration of Mennonites from the Palatinate and from Switzerland to eastern Pennsylvania began in 1709 and continued until 1754. It is estimated that this first migratory wave brought between 3,000 and 5,000 Mennonites to North America. They came to gain religious liberty and improve their economic situation.

The second migratory movement, that extended from 1815 to 1861, brought almost 3,000 persons, primarily from Switzerland and Germany. These immigrants settled in western Pennsylvania, Ohio, Indiana, Illinois, and Iowa. They came to North America to escape both the European militarism and the deplorable economic conditions produced by the Napoleonic Wars.

The other two waves came from Russia between 1873 and 1880. During this era almost 10,000 Russian Mennonites settled in North and South Dakota, Nebraska, Kansas, and Minnesota, and some 8,000 in Manitoba, in western Canada. After World War I some 18,000 more settled in Canada.

Presently 340,000 baptized Mennonites live in North America, about 70 percent in the United States and 30 percent in Canada. North America has become the second world for Mennonites.

Almost all Mennonites who live in North America are English-speaking, with the exception of a few recent European immigrants, and the congregations formed for Spanish-speaking persons or for Native Americans.

Mennonites of North America are divided into various groups with considerable variety in religious doctrine and practice. The largest of these groups is the Mennonite Church, with 1,300 congregations and 110,000 members. The Mennonite Church has certain distinctive characteristics: a strong emphasis on keeping the faith; a fervent program of missionary activities, publications, educational programs, and mutual aid; a profound faith in nonresistance (Mennonites refuse to participate in any type of military activity); and a simple lifestyle and simplicity in their form of worship (it is simple and reverent, avoiding all pomp and emotionalism).

An important leader, John H. Oberholtzer (1809-95), due to his ideas, progressive for their time, (not wearing the "plain coat," keeping minutes and writing constitutions), was excommunicated by the Franconia Mennonite Conference in 1847. He took a good number of members with him and founded the General Conference Mennonite Church, a movement whose objective was not to create still another group but to unite all North American Mennonites. Today this branch has some 28,000 members in Canada and about 37,000 in the United States, the majority of which came from Russia. This group has shown much interest in missionary and educational work, including efforts among the Native Americans in Arizona and Montana.

The third group in numerical size is the Mennonite Brethren, which originated as a spiritual renewal and revival movement in 1860 in Russia. The first Mennonite Brethren arrived in North America in 1873 and settled in Kansas. These differ from the first two groups in several ways: they use immersion as the form of baptism (the others use pouring), and they emphasize evangelistic and mission work (today they have more members in other countries than in North America). They presently have some 40,000 members in North America.

In addition to these three principal groups there are others of less importance, either for their small membership or, in the case of this study, for their lack of participation in the Hispanic work in North America. They are the following: the Old Order Amish, the Brethren in Christ, the Old Order Mennonite, the Evangelical Mennonite Brethren, the Evangelical Mennonite Church, the Krimmer Mennonite Brethren, the Evangelical Mennonite Conference, the Reformed Mennonite, the Hutterites, and the Church of God in Christ, Mennonite.

In spite of the existence of so many Mennonite groups, they largely agree on several points: that the New Testament rejects violence and the participation in military activities; that the Christian life is to be a simple life, that does not imitate societies' values; and that baptism is to be administered only to those who have accepted Christ (not to children who are saved without baptism). However, there are differences of opinion about Sunday school, the adoption of modern means of transportation and communication, and dress.

The first Mennonites that arrived in North America were not outstanding in their evangelistic or missionary spirit. Although they did not have the problems that they had faced in the Old World, their position as colonists and pioneers forced them to employ their energies in the strenuous battle against the hostile environment that surrounded them. This fact led them to develop a religious life limited to their own circle. The use of German as their means of communication together with the attachment to their customs helped reinforce this isolation. The decline in evangelistic and missionary interest that had begun in the Old World after the first generations of Mennonites, continued a similar pattern in North America.

However, the interest in evangelism among North American Mennonites was resurrected in the latter part of the nineteenth century. This "Great Awakening," as J. C. Wenger calls it, was due in large measure to the two key figures in the contemporary Mennonite Church: John F. Funk (1835-1930) and John S. Coffman (1848-99). Funk was the most influential personality in the founding and promotion of Sunday schools. He also founded the magazine *Herald of Truth* in 1864. Coffman, meanwhile, emphasized the need for mission work and evangelism. In addition, he was the principal force in the founding, in 1895, of the Elkhart Institute (today called Goshen College).

During this period a variety of activities in the North American Mennonite Church were begun. Organizations appeared dedicated to promote youth and women's activities, education, the benefits of Bible study, publications, evangelism, and missions.

It was under this banner of evangelism-mission that several things occurred of primary importance for the development of the Hispanic Mennonite work in North America. The Mennonite Board of Charities was organized in 1890 and later was combined with the Mennonite Board of Evangelism of the United States. In 1893 as a result of the work of this board the Chicago Home Mission, the first urban Mennonite mission, was established. This first effort seemed to stimulate missionary interest, and works were established in India in 1899 and Argentina in 1917.

It is interesting to note that two of these three missionary steps played an important part in the beginning of the Hispanic Mennonite work in North America: the Chicago Home Mission and the work in Argentina.[3] This Mennonite contact with the urban world and the interaction with Spanish-speaking persons[4] will be of vital importance, since they prepared the terrain for the beginnings of what will be known as the Hispanic Mennonite Church of North America.

J. W. Shank

T. K. Hershey

Elvin Snyder

Mario Bustos, Sr.

Mario de Orive

Guillermo Torres

Mac Bustos

José A. Santiago

Lupe De León

Arnoldo Casas

José M. Ortiz

Artemio de Jesús

Conrado Hinojosa

Ambrosio Encarnación

Teófilo Ponce

Samuel Hernández

Lupe García

Ronald Collins

Rafael Ramos

Mary Bustos

Seferina De León

Gladys Widmer

26

THE BEGINNINGS

2
THE BEGINNINGS

Mennonites, as we have already mentioned in the last chapter, established their first mission work in Chicago in 1893. This developed through many slow steps. The desire for a work of this nature had been simmering for a long time in the hearts of several young Mennonites who lived in the "Windy City." Some had come seeking work, but the majority were students in a variety of academic institutions such as the University of Chicago, Northwestern University, Moody Bible Institute, and several medical schools. These young people felt the need for a place in which to share and worship with persons of their own faith. In addition they saw the streets full of people in need of the message of the Word of God.

While this was happening in the city, a discussion was going on in several rural churches concerning the need for mission work. By the 1880s several important leaders were proclaiming that meeting this need was an integral part of the church's ministry. Thus by 1890 those interested persons were ready to take action. Dr. S. D. Ebersole, a Mennonite doctor who had a clinic in Chicago, was one of the principal instruments in facilitating the work in the great metropolis. This doctor believed in the need for mission work in Chicago and went about stirring up interest among the leaders of the church.

In 1892, in the first Mennonite Sunday School Conference held in Clinton Frame Mennonite Church, near Goshen, Indiana, the theme of missions was discussed but no concrete agreement resulted from this discussion. However, it was a beginning and prepared the ground for the future establishment of the mission.

In 1893, in a meeting in Zion Mennonite Church, near Bluffton, Ohio, Dr. Ebersole took a firm stand on the urgency of opening a work in Chicago. He based his argument on the great need that existed among the urban population and the opportunity that this presented for Christian workers to spread the gospel. It was finally agreed to establish a mission in Chicago. Dr. Ebersole was asked to look for an appropriate location and a secretary and treasurer of the new project were named.

They proceeded to search for a site and located the first floor of a building at 145 West 18th Street. The building was rented November 20, 1893, and inaugurated December 3.[1] The plan was to use the rooms for Sunday school, a free clinic, evangelistic meetings, and Sunday services. In addition a kindergarten was to be opened for children 3 to 6 years old.

In 1919 the Chicago Home Mission moved to 1907 South Union Avenue, where it came in contact with the Mexicans who lived in that area. Those who initiated the work never imagined that they would have contact with other ethnic groups, such as the Mexicans, who were moving into the communities previously occupied by European groups. Thousands of Mexican immigrants settled in Illinois in the first three decades of this century. These not only immigrated to Chicago, but also to surrounding cities such as Gary and Burns Harbor, Indiana, and Calumet. The majority came from the Mexican states of Jalisco, Guanajuato, and Michoacán. These immigrants came seeking better living conditions and economic security. They obtained work on the railroads, in steel foundries, and in packing houses in the principal cities of the state. The majority lived in Chicago in deplorable conditions, many of them in a sector located one mile from the Chicago Home Mission.

These Latin American immigrants transplanted their lifestyle to Chicago and, as had other groups such as the Poles, Germans, and Italians, created their own colonies in different sectors of the city. The Mexican "barrio" was outside of the region directly influenced by the Mennonite work and very few lived in the neighborhood of the Chicago Home Mission.

However, there were always the exceptions, persons that settled in sectors not dominated by their respective ethnic group. Among these exceptions were Manuel and Ignacia León who had come from Mexico with their large family in 1928 and rented an apartment near the Chicago Home Mission.

Although the family was Catholic, they attended the Spanish services of the Pentecostal Church in their community. Mr. León, who worked for a railroad company, had questions about his religion. He enjoyed the theological freedom of the Protestant Church in contrast with the rigidity of the Roman Catholic beliefs.

As part of the mission program, the workers of the Chicago Home Mission went from house to house in the surrounding community inviting the people to come to the church. One day in 1929 the León sisters were playing in front of their house when two mission workers, Emma Oyer and Anna Yordy, approached and invited them to come to church. They entered their home and asked their parents to let them attend the worship services and Sunday school. Although the parents indicated that they were Catholics, they consented to let their children attend the Mennonite Church. In this way the children of the León family began to attend Sunday school regularly. They went after having attended Catholic Mass. Since the children knew both languages, they understood the classes and felt accepted by the church. The parents, seeing the interest of their children, became interested also and began to attend. But language problems soon emerged. Because of his work, Mr. León knew a little English and could understand some of the service but Mrs. León knew no English and received no benefit. This kept them from attending with the regularity they desired.

Although they attended the Mennonite Church, the Leóns continued to be closely tied to the Catholic tradition. Several of the children were taking catechism and were planning to make their first communion. A nun that was visiting them one day became very angry when she learned of their relationship with the Protestant Church and she told them to decide between the Catholic Church or the Mennonite.

The Leóns had to make a serious decision but it was not very difficult, since the love and acceptance that they felt in the Chicago Home Mission had won their hearts. In addition, the emphasis on Bible study in the Mennonite Church helped them decide. The transition was not extremely difficult since they did not live in the Hispanic community, where expectations would have been different.

In this manner the León family became the first Mexican family to attend the Chicago Home Mission regularly. But language continued to be an impediment to the parents' regular attendance. Since they were interested in the Mennonite doctrine, they expressed their eagerness to have services in Spanish at the Home Mission.

In the meantime the León children had been inviting their friends and other children to attend Sunday school. As a result, after two years there were about a dozen Spanish-speaking children attending the services of the Chicago Home Mission. The Hispanic group continued to grow but the language difficulty remained. The children continued to come because they understood English, but although they were interested, the parents felt inhibited by the language barrier. None of the leaders at the Home Mission understood Spanish.

It was at this moment in history, 1932, that the results of two Mennonite missions, the one in Argentina and the one in Chicago, came together to mark the beginning of the Hispanic Mennonite work in North America. In 1932, J. W. Shank, a Mennonite missionary on furlough from Argentina went to Chicago to enroll at Bethany Biblical Seminary and decided to live at the Chicago Home Mission. He had been in Argentina since 1917 and in those fifteen years had become familiar with the Hispanic culture and language. His knowledge of Spanish and his interest in Hispanics led him to dedicate many of his weekends to visiting the León family and other families of the children who attended Sunday school.

These contacts with the Hispanics of Chicago, together with their desire to worship in Spanish, led Shank to begin Spanish services and invite all the Spanish-speaking persons that he knew. The first of these services was held in September of 1932. They were held Tuesday evenings in one of the rooms of the Chicago Home Mission.

Shank and Mr. León went out into the Mexican community inviting people to attend. He had obtained the addresses of a dozen children that attended Sunday school and visited their families. Through these families it became possible to reach others.

Enthusiasm for the Spanish services increased and in a short time the attendance fluctuated between 30 and 70 persons. The Hispanics rejoiced greatly in hearing the gospel preached in their own language. The growth was so great that the personnel of the Chicago Home Mission soon became concerned about the inconveniences that the Mexican people might cause. It was clear that they wanted the group to grow, but they were worried about leadership, additional expenses, and its relationship to the English-speaking church.

The group grew under Shank's leadership, but then in the summer of 1933, he had to return to Argentina. They insisted that something should be done to continue the Spanish services. Again there was a connection with the Mennonite work in Latin America when Nelson Litwiller, a missionary in Argentina who was in Goshen, Indiana, on furlough, consented to give leadership. Litwiller traveled to Chicago each week to direct the work until a permanent leader could be found. He preached there for the first time on October 1, 1933.

Due to his other commitments, the involvement of Litwiller was limited. Because of this and because he thought that the work should continue, he tried to obtain a permanent leader. Manuel León informed Litwiller of a young Mexican man who sometimes preached in the Pentecostal Church and who was praying that the Lord would guide him to a definite work among his people. One Sunday, Litwiller went to the Pentecostal Church to hear this young preacher, David Castillo, and was impressed with his ability. This led him to invite Castillo to share the leadership of the Hispanic group. Castillo accepted the invitation and immediately began to play an important part in the development of the work.[2]

Undoubtedly, Litwiller saw in Castillo a promising leader for the Hispanic group. Since Castillo was not well acquainted with Mennonite doctrine, Litwiller made arrangements for him to take a theological course at Goshen College in January 1934. Already by February, Castillo was capably leading the group. Thus David Castillo became the first Hispanic pastor in the Hispanic Mennonite Church of North America.

Before Castillo arrived several of those who attended had expressed interest in being baptized and becoming members of the Mennonite Church. Now that they had a Hispanic leader and everything was developing well, they were even more impatient in their desire to be baptized. Therefore, on Sunday, April 29, 1934, 100 persons gathered for the first baptism service in the Hispanic group. The service was a new experience for the English-speaking persons present and for the bishop who led the ceremony: the service was all in Spanish and the nine persons baptized were all from Mexico. Only eighteen months after J. W. Shank had begun worship services in Spanish, nine persons were baptized and the first Hispanic Mennonite congregation in North America was established.[3]

The embryonic Hispanic Mennonite Church continued to meet in the facilities of the Chicago Home Mission and was included in the annual budget. In reality, the new church was a subdivision of the Chicago Home Mission, because, in addition to the above, it was supervised by the Chicago Home Mission superintendent. But the Hispanic group gradually acquired its own identity.

Several reasons led the Hispanic group to look for another place to meet. The most obvious were the limited space and the distance from the Mexican community (the Chicago Home Mission was about a mile away). To these reasons was added that of racial tensions. Several English-speaking children stopped coming because there were Mexican children in their classes. Several of the workers had had little or no intercultural experience and were not prepared for such a situation. To this was added the problem of scheduling. Since the Hispanic group held their worship services Sunday afternoon, between the services of the Chicago Home Mission, the time they could use the facilities was limited.

To all of this we must add that the language problem continued. The majority of those who attended the church were recent immigrants from Mexico. Therefore they spoke little English which made it difficult for them to enter fully into the total church program.

Thus they decided that the congregation should move. It was understood that it would not become completely independent, but would maintain close connections with the Home Mission. The leadership of the Chicago Home Mission hoped that some of them would preach in English at least once a week in order to reach persons who were not Spanish speaking.

The moment for separation finally arrived. In September 1934, through the efforts of Castillo and Edwin Weaver, the superintendent of the Home Mission, they found a building for rent in the Mexican sector. The Mennonite Board of Missions approved the move and the Illinois Mennonite Conference promised to subsidize the project. Everything was ready and that same September they held their first worship services at 1128 South Halstead Street. From the beginning they carried out the plan of also holding services in English. Later, in 1935, they moved to 931 West Roosevelt.

The work continued to grow under the leadership of Castillo and his wife, Elsa, the daughter of J. W. Shank. In August 1940, Castillo left for Colorado to pastor a Hispanic Mennonite mission in the city of La Junta. This event marked the end of a lovely and significant period in the history of the church. Lester T. Hershey, who had grown up in Argentina where his parents were missionaries, replaced Castillo. During his leadership, the work continued its accelerated growth. After seven years of service in Chicago, Hershey left with his family to serve in the Mennonite work in Puerto Rico, where he was to reside for more than thirty years.

During the leadership of Hershey, specifically in 1942, the Mexican Mission officially changed its name to La Iglesia Menonita Mexicana (the Mexican Mennonite Church). This illustrates the spirit of self-understanding of the group. They did not think of themselves as a mission extension of the Chicago Home Mission, but as a congregation with all the rights and privileges of the same. (The church was also known as La Iglesia Evangélica Menonita, the Evangelical Mennonite Church.)

Also during his pastorate, Hershey founded the news bulletin, *El Heraldo Mexicano (The Mexican Herald)*. He was not satisfied with reaching only the immediate community. In the first edition, dated March 1941, he announced that it was not intended only for the Mexican Americans of Chicago but for Mexican Americans in general. In the beginning, the bulletin was mimeographed, but beginning with the November 1942 edition several changes were made: it was printed and the name changed to *El Heraldo Evangélico (The Evangelical Herald)*, so that it would appeal to all Spanish speakers in the United States. It then joined with *La Voz Menonita (The Mennonite Voice)*, of Argentina, to form *El Discípulo Cristiano (The Christian Disciple)*, published for the Latin American world in general. This specific act together with the many workers who would go out to establish new works, are proofs of the broad vision of this first Hispanic Mennonite Church.

In August 1950, in its search for better facilities in which to develop its work, the congregation purchased its own building at 1014 South Blue Island. This building, dedicated in October 1952, provided the opportunity for the congregation to establish roots. They made good use of the ample facilities that they now enjoyed: worship services were held on the first floor; the second and third floors were renovated for the use of the pastor and mission workers; and a church family lived on the fourth floor. Later, the congregation bought the two adjoining buildings and converted them into recreation areas and apartments.

In Blue Island the congregation developed a new focus. They began to hold services in English and Spanish on Sunday mornings. The membership continued to grow, perhaps due both to the bilingual services and to the visibility and accessibility of the church in its new location.

The period on Blue Island was the time of major growth and activity in the history of this church. After a time with interim pastors (Parke Lantz, Elvin Snyder, and Frank Ventura, among others), Mario Snyder was named pastor in 1953, followed by Don Brenneman in 1958. As the congregation grew it made plans to build a church building at the intersection of Blue Island Avenue and Taylor Street. But these dreams were never realized since the buildings in that sector were to be torn down to make way for the construction of the Circle Campus of the University of Illinois. Although there were many protests by members of the community, they all had to find other places to live and the Mexican Mennonite Church had to find a new home.

In 1964 the Hispanic congregation bought the Lawndale Baptist Church building located at 2520 South Lawndale Avenue. This provided the congregation with its first location that had been constructed as a church building. The congregation chose this location because it had members living in the area, and 18th and 26th Streets had come to have a predominantly Hispanic character, which they still have today. The group was to be known from this time on as the

Lawndale Mennonite Church.

During the first year the congregation had to arrange its program around the schedule of the Baptist group because they continued to use the building while their new building in Berwyn was being completed. For this reason it took time for the congregation to stabilize and develop a solid program of activities.

In spite of the magnificent and spacious facilities that the church now had, they have never been filled to capacity. After the move from Blue Island, many of the members moved to suburbs such as Maywood and Lombard. Living this far from the church interfered with their regular attendance. The present membership of the Lawndale Mennonite Church is 96.

Many pastors have served in this first Hispanic Mennonite church. The majority have been missionaries in Spanish-speaking countries, sons of missionaries, or persons that have served in Voluntary Service in Spanish-speaking countries. In addition to the ones already mentioned, Shank, Litwiller, Castillo, Hershey, Lantz, E. Snyder, M. Snyder, Ventura, and Brenneman, there are others who have given leadership to this church and therefore merit mention. These are: Orley Swartzentruber, John Litwiller, William Hallman, Neftali Torres, Weldon Martin, Ronald Collins, and Paul Leichty.

The present pastor is Hector Vázquez, who was installed October 10, 1982. Vázquez is a graduate of the Hispanic Ministries Department of Goshen College. The naming of Vázquez is significant because he is only the fourth Hispanic pastor that the church has had. And even more interesting, he is the only Hispanic after David Castillo that has been named as a permanent pastor, since Ventura was an interim pastor and Torres was an assistant pastor. It is note worthy that there were 42 years between these two Hispanic pastors.

Reviewing the list of active members of the congregation we find names of persons that have been part of the church for a long time: Ventura, Valtierra, Bean. One of them, however, is outstanding: Rose Morales. Rose is the little girl that in 1929 was playing in front of her home and was invited to the Chicago Home Mission by the mission workers Oyer and Yordy. She is the daughter of Manuel and Ignacia León. Today, more than half a century later, she continues to attend the church that she has seen come to life, develop, and complete fifty significant years of life. The Lawndale Mennonite Church has been a rich source of leaders. From its pulpit and pews have come true men of God who have been an inspiration for the Spanish-speaking Mennonite people. Among them are the names of Mac Bustos, Mario Bustos, Raúl Tadeo, John Ventura, Teófilo Ponce, and Ruperto Guedea, to name only a few.

Among the Hispanic Mennonite Churches of North America, Lawndale has a unique characteristic: it is a bilingual congregation. Its worship services are held first in Spanish and then in English. On special occasions bilingual services are held where both groups participate together. Sunday school is taught in English for the children and in both languages for the adults. Sunday evening worship services are in Spanish and Wednesday evening Bible studies are held in community homes in Spanish.

There are several activities for which the church merits special recognition. One is the Lawndale Choir. It was formed in the late seventies under the direction of Arlen Hershberger. Its repertoire included both popular and religious songs in English and Spanish. This group, which was originally organized to raise funds for church needs, traveled to many states and visited a large number of Mennonite Churches. Before dissolving, the group recorded a lovely album titled "Everything Is Beautiful."

Another activity in which Lawndale has been involved is the Fresh-Air Program. This was established by the Chicago Home Mission to provide the opportunity for urban children to spend two weeks of the summer living on farms with Mennonite families. These children, whose train fare was paid for them, went to farms in Indiana, Illinois, and Iowa for the purpose of living in totally rural surroundings. The program was not limited to Lawndale but included other urban Mennonite churches. (The first group of children was sent to Sterling, Illinois, in 1896.) This program has helped the Mennonite Church make contact with Hispanics and many have come to church through this route.

Presently the church serves the community in a variety of ways: a primary school, the Chicago Mennonite Learning Center; a summer program to complement the education of the children of the community; and a seminar on contemporary family issues.

In March 1981, the Lawndale Mennonite Church developed congregational goals that indicate the enterprising and renewing spirit that it maintains after 50 years of history. Among these goals are the following: "That Lawndale Mennonite Church have a strong youth program and that each person be a spiritually growing member of a spiritually growing fellowship."

On August 7-8, 1982, the church celebrated its fiftieth anniversary. The evening of the seventh they held a banquet and a special program. Lupe Bustos reflected on the years at the Chicago Home Mission, Ida Habermehl and Dorothy Bean talked about the years as the Mexican Mennonite Church, and Mary Valtierra shared memories of Lawndale Mennonite Church. Gifts of appreciation were given to Habermehl and Bean in recognition of their many years of service. Lester T. Hershey, pastor of the church from 1940 to 1947, preached on the theme, "God Has Made Us Grow," based on 1 Corinthians 3:8. A heavy rain and three inches of water in the church basement did not dampen the celebration; they enjoyed the fellowship and ate the meal in the sanctuary.

In the Sunday morning service, August 8, another of the early leaders of the Hispanic group, Nelson Litwiller, brought the message and the children of Manuel and Ignacia León sang several special numbers. In addition to Hershey and Litwiller, the activities included the presence of David Castillo, William Hallman, and Ronald Collins.

The celebration of the fiftieth anniversary was a landmark in the history of the church, because it marks the dedication and perseverance of the Hispanic Mennonites. In spite of racial, linguistic, and cultural problems they have known how to identify with and remain Mennonite and Hispanic. This determined and competitive spirit of the first Hispanic Mennonite Church of North America will be the distinctive mark of the many others that will begin and develop in the next decades.[4]

YEARS OF THRUST AND ORGANIZATION

3
YEARS OF THRUST AND ORGANIZATION

From its beginning in 1932 the Hispanic church began to develop in other parts of the North American continent and during the decades from 1940 to 1960 congregations were established in Texas, Pennsylvania, New York, Ohio, and Iowa. But this development was slow and decentralized. Thus the church did not reach its full thrust until the last of the sixties nor its full organization until the decade of the seventies. It was during these years that the church obtained the qualities that would shake it from its lethargy: solidarity, self-identity, and organization.

In North America, in the time between the beginning of the Hispanic Mennonite Church and its awakening in the last few years, it lived in an environment of racial discrimination. In 1956, in Montgomery, Alabama, Martin Luther King, Jr., began his movement to obtain civil rights. This movement was a struggle against racial discrimination using the tactics of social demands and nonviolence. The black, Chicano, and Native American power movements began in this era. In the beginning these movements were known by their slogans, "Black is beautiful" and "Viva la raza," but between 1964 and 1968 in the major cities of the United States a chain of social riots broke out with much loss of life and property.

These events began to disturb the leaders of the Mennonite minorities. Already by 1956 the church, through the Mennonite

43

Central Committee, had explored ways in becoming involved in the social problems of minorities[1] but it was not until 1968 that something specific was done. In that year a meeting of pastors was held in Elkhart, Indiana, to draw up a position statement on these pressing social problems. The theme of formulating goals and objectives for the work ahead predominated in this meeting. At the same time they sought to understand the Black Power movement and its relationship to the concept of brotherhood in the Mennonite Church. Vern Miller, Anglo pastor of an integrated (white and black) congregation in Cleveland, Ohio, presented a document that proposed the formation of an Afro-American Council. After much discussion, Ernest Bennett, executive secretary of the Mennonite Board of Missions, agreed to include this in the agenda of the annual meeting of that agency, to be held in Kidron, Ohio.

In this meeting, held July 3-5, 1968, it was agreed to call together all of the minority Mennonite churches. A resolution was presented stating the position of the Mennonite Church on the problem of racism. The document presented the following resolutions: that each person confess his sins of pride concerning his social, racial, and cultural position; that every person be recognized as an equal; that more information about minority groups be compiled; that everything possible be done to help blacks with financial and human resources; that minority leadership be utilized; and that conversations be initiated with Mennonite blacks in order to understand the problems of minority groups.

This initial step, although planned and elaborated principally for blacks, was of vital importance for minorities in general. In the specific case of Hispanics, now, after 36 years of existence, the doors of the principal denominational structures were being opened.

The first meeting of delegates from all the minority congregations was held in Chicago during the first days of October 1968. The delegates decided the following: (1) to organize an Urban Racial Council, and (2) to elect an executive committee composed of five persons. This executive committee would direct the implementation of the Urban Racial Council. In addition the committee would determine the policy and philosophy of the work of the council and name an executive secretary to direct development of the program.

The executive committee selected was composed of Gerald Hughes, president, Lee Roy Berry, John Powell, Hubert Schwartz-entruber, and John Ventura (the only Hispanic). This committee appointed John Powell, who at that time pastored the Tenth Street Mennonite Church in Wichita, Kansas, as executive secretary of the council. In November 1969, Powell began to exercise his administrative functions from the offices of the Mennonite Board of Missions. As far as we have been able to determine, this made him the first minority administrator in the Mennonite Church.

The Hispanics present in this historic meeting expressed their appreciation for the fact that it was not necessary for them to become an integral part of the council. However, they thought that they should be observers and assist in whatever way possible to support the blacks. The Hispanics thought that there was discrimination against blacks but not against Mexican-Americans. (It should be noted, however, that there was a good representation of Hispanics present in this meeting.)

The first meeting of the recently formed executive committee of the Urban Racial Council was held in January 1969. This meeting produced several issues of great importance for the evolutionary development of the Hispanic agenda. The most important was the creation of a council analogous to that of the blacks. This council would work directly with the agenda of the Hispanic Mennonite community.

Finally, for the first time in the history of the church, Mennonite Hispanics met in Chicago on December 5 and 6, 1969. The group decided that the needs of the Hispanic brotherhood could be met by the present group, but that there should be some structural changes. They appointed a committee of five persons consisting of Griselda Garza, Sammy Santos, John Ventura, Mac Bustos, and Teodoro Chapa which would serve as a unifying link between the Hispanic community and the executive committee of the Urban Racial Council. The Hispanics were not interested in creating another organization. They only wanted to become a part of the present organization but with two recommendations for change: the quantitative representation of the Hispanic group and the name of the council. The first recommendation would equalize the black and Hispanic representation on the executive committee of the council. The second recommendation was to change the name to one that would represent the integration of two groups that, although minorities, had different problems.

Thus, during its meeting on January 9 and 10, 1970, the council recommended that the name of the organization be changed to better reflect the minority problems of the Mennonite brotherhood. It was felt that the name, Urban Racial Council, only represented the concerns of the urban blacks and that a change was needed to consolidate all concerns. Therefore, from that moment the name, Minority Ministries Council, was adopted.

During March 1971, the council asked that the Hispanics name a candidate for the position of associate secretary. In July of that same year Lupe De León, from Mathis, Texas, was appointed to fill that position. Thus De León became the first Hispanic to occupy a strategic administrative position in the central structure of the Mennonite Church. De León worked together with Powell for the interests of the minorities, but in particular, he worked for the development of the Hispanic agenda.

This significant appointment paved the way for others that would strengthen the employment of Hispanics. In 1972 Neftalí Torres, after having served as copastor of the Lawndale Mennonite Church, was employed by the newly created Mennonite Board of Congregational Ministries to work in the area of literature, family life, and peace. During the same year Teodoro Chapa was appointed coordinator of the first Cross-Cultural Youth Convention.

From its inception the council worked in many areas, such as the development and administration of new welfare programs and projects in minority communities and congregations, the struggle for identity, the identification and employment of human and physical resources, and the racial conscience-raising of the minority churches. In this way the council became involved in the economic development at both the congregational and conference level and in special projects such as the Congregational Health Insurance Plan that was carried out in cooperation with Mennonite Mutual Aid. From the beginning the council also worked as an advocate and voice for the interests and concerns of the minority Mennonite churches.

After several years it became evident that there was a duplication of services between the council and other agencies, especially the Home Missions Department.[2] In addition to this duplication, it was thought that it would be profitable for the Mennonite Church in general to make use of the services of minority personnel. Also, there existed the concern that budgets would be used more effectively if there were some central structure that would administer all the funds of both divisions.

With these factors in mind a committee was selected to study the issue and bring their recommendations. This committee was composed of Atlee Beechy and Samuel Janzen, appointed by the Mennonite Board of Missions; Vince Jamison and Warner Jackson, appointed by the Black Council of the Minority Ministries Council; John Ventura and Al Valtierra, Jr., appointed by the Hispanic Council of the Minority Ministries Council; Glen Brubacher and Hubert Schwartzentruber, appointed by the Home Missions Department; and Paul N. Kraybill, who would serve as president, appointed by the Mennonite Board of Missions. Ernest Bennett was selected by the committee to serve as secretary. The committee brought the recommendation that the two organizations, the Minority Ministries Council and Home Missions, a division of the Mennonite Board of Missions be joined. This would become the central issue in the Fifth Annual Assembly of the Minority Ministries Council held in Sandía, Texas.

This long anticipated important meeting was held October 19 to 21, 1973, and became a major milestone in the history of the Hispanic church and made Sandía a symbolic word for the participants in this meeting. Six local Hispanic Mennonite churches served as hosts for this activity that attracted more than 160 persons. Delegates were present from some 75 minority congregations.

In the first meeting the fusion of the two organizations was discussed together with the call to name an associate secretary of Intercultural Concerns who would work with the General Board of the Mennonite Church. With this new plan a Council of Intercultural Concerns composed of blacks and Hispanics, and possibly Native Americans and French, would serve as an advisory group to the associate secretary. There were diverse reactions among the groups represented. Some doubted that only one associate secretary could repre-

sent adequately the interests of all of the minority groups. In addition
to this and other secondary concerns, the major concern was the death
of the organization that for the first time had given identity to the
minorities of the Mennonite Church.

In the beginning the black group voted against the recommendation. This was not a rejection of the idea, but simply a precaution
against possible future results. After holding separate group sessions
on Friday afternoon, a conjoint business meeting was held that evening. The Hispanic group recommended the addition of a second associate secretary: one for the Hispanic agenda and one for the black.
After a long discussion a vote was taken. The motion was approved by
a large majority.

The blacks decided to meet later to determine what steps to take
in the newly approved organization. But, in the meantime, the Hispanics took immediate action and began to organize the Hispanic
Council according to the new structure: they appointed Teodoro
Chapa and Al Valtierra, Jr., as representatives in the new Intercultural
Council; they suggested an alternative plan in case the new structure
did not materialize; they decided to collaborate with the Junta
Ejecutiva Latinoamericana de Audiciones Menonitas, JELAM (Executive Council of Latin American Mennonite Broadcasts); they accepted the idea of working with the Mennonite Publishing House and
the Mennonite Board of Congregational Ministries in the development of Bible study materials in Spanish for children and adults; and
they adopted the task of identifying books and materials for the Hispanic pastors. In addition they appointed the new Hispanic Council
composed of the following members: Mac Bustos, Iowa, president;
Maria Snyder, Kansas, secretary; Teodoro Chapa, Texas; Artemio de
Jesús, New Jersey; Guillermo Tijerina, Ohio; John Ventura, Colorado;
Guadalupe Longoria, Texas; and Al Valtierra, Jr., Illinois. These were
to meet in Chicago November 24 of that year to plan the future of the
Hispanic Mennonite Churches of North America.

This new organization made possible the direct representation of
the minority concerns to the total structure of the Mennonite Church.
In this new plan the Minority Ministries Council disappeared, but the
work that it had begun was more completely integrated into the life of
the church. In addition, the two associate secretaries would represent

in a comprehensive way the interests of the minority congregations to the conferences, the agencies of the different boards, and the interdenominational agencies. The economic development of the churches would be transferred to Home Missions.

In addition, in this meeting, a series of significant recommendations were made: that the boards and agencies of the Mennonite Church plan to involve minority persons; that priority be given to minorities when personnel are sought, especially in strategic areas such as Home Missions; that the Coordinating Council of the General Board be responsible for coordinating the strategy of church growth for North America, and that the two associate secretaries of Minority Concerns be made members of said council.

Sandía 73 has had a tremendous impact in many aspects. Before this event the Hispanic church lacked self-identity because it largely depended on the English-speaking church. After the reorganization, however, it began to function as an institution with its own identity. From this moment, the Hispanic Mennonites could think of a body that represented them and which would fight for their interests in the central structure of the denomination.

The Hispanics made good use of the Sandía meeting to celebrate their first Workers Retreat, October 14-18, 1973. Sixty-five persons from Colorado, Iowa, Illinois, Indiana, Ohio, Pennsylvania, New York, New Jersey and Oregon attended this activity. There were additional representatives from Mexico and Puerto Rico. This became the first of a series that continue to the present. Except for the meeting in December 1969, in Chicago, which was really on a much smaller scale, there had not been an activity of this nature before this retreat.

In this meeting certain basic priorities for the development of the Hispanic Mennonite people were identified whose effects are still felt. One of the items that received major attention was the need for literature in Spanish. The following recommendation was made: Sunday school material be provided for children and adolescents, material be provided for Bible schools, collaboration in the production of a Spanish hymnal, and the various Mennonite periodicals publish articles in Spanish.

Priority was also given to ministerial concerns with the following recommendations: an intensive effort be made to have Hispanic pastors for Hispanic congregations; state and regional workshops be held directed by minority personnel in areas such as counseling, leadership developed into the Hispanic Ministries Department at Goshen College. lines of communication between conferences, the Board of Missions, and pastors be established so that the pastors know to whom they should direct their concerns; to ask that pastors not be dismissed without a hearing and an evaluation of the situation and that one member of the Hispanic Council be present for said proceedings; and the situation of housing, income, etc., of all pastors be reviewed.

Other aspects that received attention in order of priority were: the role of women in the Hispanic church, a youth conference for minorities, the development of a seminary for Hispanic leadership training, the commitment of the General Board to include more Hispanic representation in the different boards, increased publicity for farm workers and their misfortunes, college recruitment, the need for a youth secretary under the Mennonite Board of Congregational Ministries, the Hispanic representation on the Student Services Committee, the need for high schools in the large cities and the need for orientation for writing proposals for opening day-care centers.

Finally, in June of 1974 the model established in Sandía became a reality. Lupe De León was appointed associate secretary in the Department of Home Missions and José M. Ortiz, associate general secretary of Latin Concerns under the General Board. The Office of Latin Concerns was opened in August 1974 in Rosemont, Illinois, and in 1977 was moved to Elkhart. The establishment of these two positions, that were directed specifically to the Hispanic agenda, would be crucial for the development of the church.

A large part of the agenda of the Hispanic Council in that year concerned the integration of Hispanic personnel into the agencies, boards, committees and projects of the Mennonite Church. In this way Hispanics would have voice and vote in the decisions that would directly affect their people.

The idea of an institute on wheels was also one of the issues that received much time and attention in that year. A committee was appointed to plan such a project composed of Lupe De León, Mac Bustos, Guillermo Tijerina, Artemio de Jesús, and José M. Ortiz, plus representation from the churches of Pennsylvania consisting of José A.

Santiago and Benjamín Pérez. This was the initiative that later developed into the Hispanic Ministries Department at Goshen College.

During this period, work was begun on the project to write a constitution for all of the Hispanic Mennonite Churches in North America. A committee composed of José A. Santiago, Caonabo Reyes, and José M. Ortiz was appointed to begin this work. They would prepare a draft that after having been revised by the Hispanic Council would be presented at the Second Workers Retreat in April 1975.

In that year there emerged a longing for better communication between the churches. An informative paper, *El Noticiero* (The Reporter), began publication, edited by José M. Ortiz and Artemio de Jesús. A committee was appointed composed of Mary Bustos, Frank Ventura, Lupe García, Caonabo Reyes, Arnoldo Casas, and Guillermo Espinoza to work with literature needs in Spanish. These were the initial steps that led to the magazine known today as *Ecos Menonitas* (Mennonite Echoes).

Already in this year there was tremendous interest in programs "by and for Hispanics": literature, education, etc. In addition, the fact that a constitution was being written indicated the determined attitude of the group to have their own regulations and goals, to have their own conscience and purpose, to be concerned about "what is ours."

In 1975 the Second Workers Retreat was held June 23-26 at Camp Hebron, Halifax, Pennsylvania. This event was extremely important because it gave continuity to the tradition established in Sandía in 1973 and demonstrated the desire for solidarity, self-identity, and organization that the Hispanic Mennonite conglomerate possessed. They adopted as the theme for the event, "Tomorrow is today . . . for the Hispanic Mennonite Church," which clearly implied the desire for immediate and determined effort. A very significant hymn was chosen as a theme for the occasion, "Anunciaremos tu Reino" (We Will Announce Your Kingdom). Among the speakers was Cecilio Arrastía speaking on "Identifying, Training, and Renewing the Hispanic Pastorate."

Among the many items on the agenda the most important was the presentation and approval of the constitution. Its preamble reads as follows:

We, the Hispanic Mennonite churches in the United States, moved by the desire to do the will of God, and with the conviction that it is imperative that we give testimony of the unity of Christ as God and only Savior, and under the direction of the Holy Spirit, do we resolve to establish the National Council of the Hispanic Mennonite churches as part of the General Board of the Mennonite Church.[3]

Following this impressive and challenging preamble it proceeds to present twelve articles titled as follows: name, address, doctrinal position and administration, purpose, membership, administrative committee, permanent commissions, temporary commissions, interdenominational relationships, amendments, quorum, rules of order, power of dissolution, and escape clause. Among these articles the objectives of the Hispanic church merit particular attention.

1. The primary purpose of this council is to promote the progress of the member churches in their pastoral, evangelistic, educational and Christian service work. For these ends it may receive and administer the necessary funds for projects and activities that it may develop, either alone or in conjunction with the agencies of the Mennonite Church.
2. To support and stimulate the agencies of our church and promote the creation and development of new ministries.
3. To create, develop, and delegate programs of action in the face of specific situations in which it is felt the council should intervene.
4. To encourage good working relations between the congregations and their pastors, facilitating opportunities for spiritual and educational edification.

The constitution indicates that this council will function on a national level and will be composed of the Hispanic Mennonite churches of North America. In addition, the document states that during the assembly the official delegates, one for every hundred members or fraction plus the pastor, will elect three members of the administrative committee. Each region of the country will elect an additional member from their region. This administrative committee will elect its president, who will represent the council when required, will sign correspondence, documents, and proclamations authorized by the committee. A vice-president will be elected to exercise the functions of the president in case of his absence or resignation, a secretary to keep the minutes, a treasurer to keep the financial records of the council, and five members at large who will serve on the program, resolutions, and findings committees. The associate secretary of Latin Concerns will be an ex-officio member of the administrative committee.

The writing and acceptance of the constitution was another sure sign of the maturity that the church had reached at that moment. Every well-structured organization needs clear, forward looking regulations. The Hispanic church had taken this step with the objective to "give witness to the unity of Christ as God and only Savior."

In 1976 several aspects were emphasized: evangelism, fraternal relations with the Mennonite churches of Puerto Rico, and interchange with black Mennonites. It was affirmed that there is a need for a new vision in the unity of Christ as a pluralistic brotherhood. Work was begun on several intercultural projects.

In addition to these issues, they worked diligently in the field of education. A committee was formed to explore the possibilities of establishing an educational center. Three educational institutions were visited: the Río Grande Bible Institute, in Edinburg, Texas; Hesston College, Hesston, Kansas; and the Nazarene Hispanic American Seminary, in San Antonio, Texas. After a time of negotiations and difficult decisions it was decided to establish a cooperative project between Hesston College and the Nazarene Hispanic American Seminary for the pastoral training of Hispanic Mennonite youth. The program would be located at the Nazarene Seminary with accreditation through Hesston College. The same committee would work in the definition of program, schedule, and budget.

Another accomplishment of this year was the establishment of the Office of Congregational Education and Literature in Spanish, created in cooperation with the Mennonite Board of Congregational Ministries and the Mennonite Publishing House. Arnoldo Casas was employed as the secretary of this office. A Commission of Congregational Education and Literature in Spanish to supervise the secretary was appointed consisting of Enriqueta Díaz, Donna Hernández, Sila Oliva, Lupe García, and Rafael Falcón.

The accomplishments of these last two steps were very important because they were the beginning of the realization of the two principal dreams of Sandía: the education of Hispanic Mennonite leadership, and literature in Spanish. Clearly these are part of a solid foundation for a bright future for the church.

In February 1977, the first Hispanic conference on immigration was held in Washington, D.C. Seeing the deplorable situation of the Hispanic immigrant the Home Missions Department of the Mennonite Board of Missions made available the services of Lupe De León to the U.S. Peace Section of the Mennonite Central Committee to organize and direct this activity. As a result of this conference the National Council was able to establish the office of Mennonite Hispanic Immigration Service in February 1978 in Washington, D.C., and appoint Karen Ventura as director.

In this same year, 1977, in a meeting held June 22-23 in Estes Park, Colorado, three candidates were nominated to direct the theological training program to be established in the Nazarene Hispanic American Seminary. Victor Alvarez was ultimately selected as director of this program and began his work in August 1977.

The National Council held its Third Workers Retreat at Hesston College August 2 to 5, 1977, for the purpose of promoting the Mennonite colleges. "Study to shew thyself approved unto God, a workman that needeth not to be ashamed, rightly dividing the word of truth" (2 Timothy 2:15) was used as the theme of this third retreat. For this occasion the associate secretary, José M. Ortiz, gave a comprehensive and challenging presentation titled "The Hispanic Mennonite Pastorate," which was a reflection on the situation of the Hispanic Mennonite people in that specific moment of their history.

The address began with a call to "develop our own structures and not copy the models of other groups." Later in the talk he pointed out the need for the development of pastors. There was an attitude of apathetic satisfaction in several practices: to use independent pastors but with a Mennonite salary; to benefit from pastoral subsidy whether or not there is congregational development, thus promoting a spirit of dependency; to neglect the responsibility to keep the conference and the National Council informed, thus demonstrating a certain degree of irresponsibility, and to rarely attend the retreats or meetings of the conference; and to operate year after year without congregational and personal goals.[5] As the solution to this situation he presented several alternatives: (1) encourage the pastors to obtain academic preparation and earn their own support; and (2) make it a requirement that pastors receiving subsidy attend the key meetings and workshops of the council, conference, or region. In addition he pointed out several urban centers that present the possibility of opening Hispanic work in the next five years. Of the seven that he mentioned only two have materialized: Los Angeles, California, and Carlsbad, New Mexico.

His presentation concluded with words filled with meanings that incited reflection on the true purpose of the Hispanic church. "I conclude these comments", said Ortiz, "by stating that to be the church is more than to develop programs, to lead in worship, to bring offerings, to ordain pastors, and commission laymen. In Anabaptist language it is to be converted into instruments of reconciliation and in the language of the Gospels it is to be converted into 'the salt of the earth and the light of the world.' That means to be faithful to Jesus and to him only offer our loyalty and our ministries."[6]

In 1977 the Mennonite Board of Missions, meeting at Kidron, Ohio, October 28-29, appointed Lupe De León to replace Simon Gingerich as secretary of Home Missions. De León who began in 1971 as associate secretary of the Minority Ministries Council and later in 1974 became the associate secretary of Home Missions, now occupied a super-strategic position in the development of the Hispanic Mennonite Church.

From August 14-18, 1978, the IV Convention (previously called Workers' Retreat) was held on the campus of Goshen College. "Affirming our faith and expressing our discipleship" was the theme of this gathering. The biblical text was, "Earnestly contend for the faith" (Jude 3). During this conference the emphasis was on the intellectual growth of the congregation. Until that moment the church had done very well in numerical growth, but now the call was made for growth in understanding. In essence the songs, programs, worship, and congregational life in general should reflect the Anabaptism that it professes. This was emphasized because of the conditions that were and still are experienced: the Sunday schools are nurtured by Nazarenes, Baptists, Pentecostals, and interdenominationals because of the lack of Anabaptist materials in Spanish; many congregations display a sign that says "Mennonite Church" but the concept reaches no farther; and, the shortage of leaders pushes congregations to hand over the flock to pastors from other denominations.

Because of this situation and other concerns the following recommendations were made:

1. The administrative committee wishes to shed its decorative role and take more initiative in the Hispanic program.

2. Theological training at the college level will have primary agenda and budget priority. The Hispanic church should commit itself to raise $5,000 for the expenses of the 1978-79 academic year.

3. There is a desire for greater integration of Hispanic personnel in Hispanic programs.

4. The Hispanic Mennonite Church of North America should serve as a missionary church in Latin America.

In addition there was dialogue about a better relationship with the English-speaking Mennonite Church. This was due to the fact that there had been a change from "missions" to autonomous congregations, and therefore the relationship was different.

Ivan Kauffmann, general secretary of the General Board of the Mennonite Church, in his report to the Assembly presented five suggestions to the Hispanic congregations, which indicate the basic points that merit attention from the point of view of the Anglo church.

1. That each congregation commit itself to the discipling mission of the Mennonite Church emphasizing both winning and training disciples.

2. That each congregation evaluate the needs that it cannot meet locally and inform its district conference.

3. That each congregation study *Affirming Our Faith in Word and Deed* before the Annual Assembly in 1979.

4. That each congregation identify persons with leadership potential that should be involved in higher education, and that each search for ways to encourage and help them to get such training.

5. That each congregation be alert to opportunities to help begin new work.[8]

The five suggestions of Kauffmann can be summarized as soul winning, training, communication, conceptual growth, and leadership. These are concerns that the Hispanic group had already emphasized or mentioned. However, in spite of the maturity already attained, his points were valid and merited close attention.

In this IV Convention of 1978, the constitution approved in the II Workers Retreat in 1975 was revised. The principle changes were in article IV pertaining to two aspects of the administrative committee: the addition of a representative appointed by the Hispanic Women's Conference, and the qualifications and duties of the president. The changes made indicated a genuine desire to give the women the opportunity to be part of a primary group of the Hispanic church.

In that same year, 1978, Federico Rosado, a recent graduate of Goshen College, directed the Cross-cultural Youth Convention. In addition, Irving Pérez was appointed director of the High-Aim program, a position he held until 1979 when he decided to study at Goshen College. Pérez was the second Hispanic to direct this program since Lupe García had been the director in 1972.

In 1979, following the recommendation of the IV Convention, the theological training program at the Nazarene Hispanic American Seminary was moved to Goshen College. Lourdes Miranda was appointed professor and Rafael Falcón, professor and director of the program. The Mennonite Central Committee employed Rolando Santiago as assistant director of programs for the United States. At the same time Ambrosio Encarnación was appointed supervisor of the Hispanic work in Florida under the auspices of the Southeast Mennonite Convention.

It is undeniable that the decade of the 70s had brought an avalanche of tremendous gains for the Hispanic Mennonite Church of North America. However, the 80s would be years of challenge with the problems already present in addition to those yet to come of a new and different era.

The activities of the present decade began with the V Convention held at Eastern Mennonite College, in Harrisonburg, Virginia, August 12-15, 1980. Some 100 persons participated in the activities that were developed around the central theme "Towards Christian Maturity."

The topics discussed focused on the concern for maturity: "produce materials on Anabaptist theology and make them accessible to the pastors and leaders, raise the consciousness of youth concerning the ways of the armed services, establish guidelines to be followed for persons who want to serve as pastors in Hispanic Mennonite churches, and move toward an independent economy in the decade of the eighties." The Mennonite Confession of Faith was discussed and on the recommendation of the assembly it was accepted with the revision of certain aspects such as the veiling of women, the role of women, and baptism.[9]

After days of discussion, decisions, and hard work the following resolutions were made:

1. That the literature committee continue to work on the preparation of Sunday school material in Spanish.

2. That the administrative committee search for ways to provide orientation for the youth in the area of nonresistance.

3. That the pastors be informed that any doubts about the recognition of their ordination should be resolved with their respective conferences.

4. That persons appointed to committees or offices in the Mennonite Church be selected on the basis of Acts 6:3.

5. That Hispanic personnel in the agencies be encouraged to attend Hispanic Mennonite churches.

6. That the National Council follow up on the themes presented by means of regional workshops.

7. That Mennonite Central Committee name an advisory committee to work with Karen Ventura.

8. That there be continued development of relations with the Hispanic brothers of Canada.[10]

Growth and Christian maturity were most appropriate themes for this convention. Undeniably the church grew and matured as it confronted new obstacles and concerns and its members sought to be faithful Christians.

June 15 of that same year one of the persons responsible for those "years of gains and development" turned over the reins of leadership. After serving for nine years as secretary of Home Missions, Lupe De León resigned his position. During his incumbency the emphasis on urban mission, ministry to the deaf, and the development of better working relations with the conferences were developed. In addition and more important for the Hispanic church, he helped establish the Office of Congregational Education and Literature in Spanish, contributed to the development of the programs of minority leadership, and incorporated the Hispanic Mennonite congregations and their leaders as part of the backbone of the denomination.[11]

On October 27-30, 1981, a meeting of considerable importance was held at Epworth Forest Campground, North Webster, Indiana. Representatives of all the Hispanic programs and agencies met to discuss the implications of a proposal to restructure the Hispanic Mennonite Church. This proposal had been presented at the General Assembly of the Mennonite Church held at Bowling Green, Ohio, during August 1981. After long and difficult discussions they reached the following conclusions: (1) to continue working with the proposal presented in the General Assembly with the intent that the Hispanic group makes its own decision; (2) to recognize that certain historical events in the Mennonite Church have mandated certain decisions; (3) to continue negotiating with the General Board and the Board of Missions for the budget of the Office of Latin Concerns of the General Board and that each regional council continue to administer its annual budget; (4) that the concept of self-sufficiency be promoted and that funds be employed in local ministries, pastoral support, and physical plant needs. The meeting concluded with the following recommendations: "that the proposal be presented in the next meeting of the National Council (November 12-14); that the document be finalized by March 1982 and be presented for acceptance or rejection in the VI Convention of the Hispanic Council in Hesston, Kansas, in August 1982."[12]

The years of thrust and organization were completed with the celebration of the fiftieth anniversary of the Hispanic Mennonite

Church of North America, held in conjunction with the VI Convention. Two hundred and twenty persons gathered for this historic activity August 13-16, 1982, at Hesston College.

Among the many important items on the agenda of these business sessions the most important was the restructuring proposal. The administrative committee presented a proposal recommending the formation of the Conference of Hispanic Mennonite churches of North America. (Note the change of National Council to Conference and the addition of "of North America.") The proposal, both in its introduction and in its six sections of identity, purpose, administration, finances and program, structural model, and constitutional document revealed a deep desire for self-determination, self-identity, and the consolidation of efforts of a purely Hispanic nature. After a prolonged discussion of finances, personnel, relationships, time, procedure, implications, etc., the Assembly recommended that a commission be appointed to continue the study of the proposal and that it be brought again for consideration in the 1984 Assembly. The commission appointed was composed of Lupe García, Andrés Gallardo, Rafael Ramos, and Ambrosio Encarnación.

As part of the celebration of the anniversary, recognition was given to several mission leaders that had dedicated part of their lives to the development of the Hispanic work. Among these persons were Lester T. Hershey, Elvin Snyder, Paul Conrad, William Hallman, and Ronald Collins. Mac Bustos gave a brief review of those 50 memorable years mentioning the names of key persons in the realization of this fruitful story.

In addition to all of this the occasion was also used to give recognition to José M. Ortiz for his eight years of service at the head of the Office of Latin Concerns. Ortiz was resigning after having left his indelible stamp on the development during these years of drive and organization. It is without question that Ortiz, together with De León, had played a principal role in the accomplishments gained in these later years. Many dreams became reality under his careful and capable leadership.[13]

As is natural in all activity of this kind, resolutions must be elaborated. In this special occasion the following resolutions were defined:

1. That the administrative committee recommend persons known in the Hispanic churches for positions in the agencies.

2. That the Mennonite Central Committee translate its program pamphlets into Spanish and distribute them in the congregations.

3. That the administrative committee recommend to the Mennonite Board of Education that it develop educational programs for pastors presently serving without jeopardizing the Hispanic Ministries Department program now in existence.

4. That a letter be sent to President Ronald Reagan in the name of the Hispanic churches concerning their position in relation to the present administration and its policies in Central America. [14]

Fifty years of Hispanic Mennonite history in North America have just been celebrated and it is obvious that the last few have been key ones for the development of the church. It has been possible to observe the leaders and the events that have made this a reality. So now with this background it would be profitable to ask, "Who will lead in the next years and what will happen?" A new era has begun and it is not known who will lead nor what will happen. However, we can be certain of one thing; that the same God who so faithfully directed the first fifty years will continue to walk ahead. [15]

One of the first congregations. La Junta, Colorado.

First Evangelical Mennonite Church of Brooklyn, when at 12 Jefferson Street.

Services in Lend-a-Hand. Davenport, Iowa, July 1962.

Meeting of the Minority Ministries Council. Chicago. 1970.

Lawndale Choir. Lawndale Mennonite Church. Chicago.

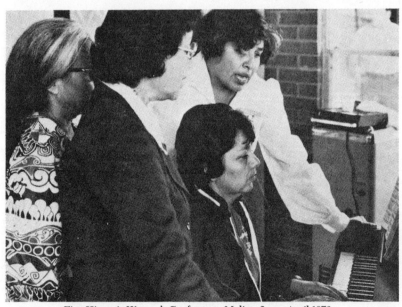

First Hispanic Women's Conference. Moline, Iowa, April 1973.

Sandía meeting. Texas, October 1973.

Left to right: José M. Oritz, Arnoldo Casas, Lupe De León, and Rafael Falcón, in 1980.

First Pastors Meeting. Goshen College, Goshen, Indiana, May 1981.

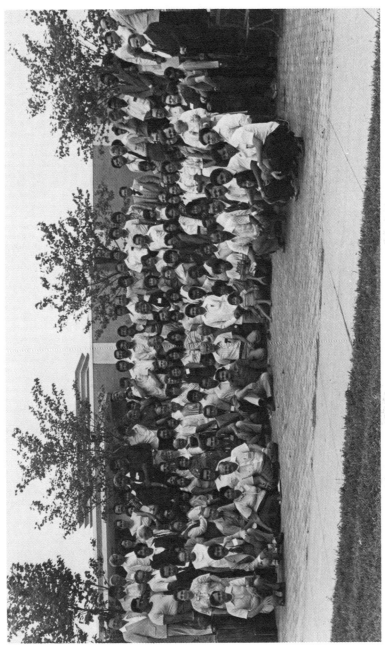

Fiftieth Anniversary. Hesston College, Hesston, Kansas, August 13-16, 1982.

THE CONGREGATIONS

4
THE CONGREGATIONS

$\mathbf{B}$y 1982 the Hispanic Mennonite Church had more than 50 congregations, home for about 2,000 members, spread in all directions over the continent. The congregations are small with an average of 35 members. They are located in Washington, D.C., and sixteen states: Texas (6), Ohio (3), Pennsylvania (9), New York (8), Iowa (2), Oregon (3), Indiana (2), Idaho, Illinois (5), Arizona, New Jersey (2), Florida (4), California (3), New Mexico, Delaware, and Michigan.

As can be seen by the numbers that appear in parenthesis after each state, Pennsylvania has the largest number of congregations, followed by New York, Texas, Illinois, and Florida. Illinois is of special interest because all of the congregations except Moline are located in Chicago. (Meanwhile, in Pennsylvania, Lancaster is the geographical center.)

The congregations are located in areas densely populated by Hispanics. If a mental map were made of the locations of these congregations clearly it could be seen that the northeastern part of the continent dominates and that there are areas such as the Northwest and West where there is almost a complete absence of congregations. Presently, in addition to these groups already established, there are several being developed: Long Beach, California; Peoria, Arizona; West Liberty, Iowa; and Harlingen, Texas. These are tangible proof of the impetus for growth and evangelism that characterizes the Hispanic Mennonite family.

In Canada, as far as we can determine, there are three congrega-

71

tions: Edmonton and Calgary in Alberta, and the recently established congregation of Montreal in Quebec. In addition there were plans to begin a work in Winnipeg in the winter of 1983. These congregations in Canada are composed primarily of brethren from Chile who recently assisted several churches in Chile to become part of the Mennonite Church.

The congregations came to life for several principal reasons: the missionary commitment of the Mennonites to develop urban missions, the immigration of Latin American Mennonites to the continent, the changes in employment for mission personnel who return from Latin America, the establishment of Voluntary Service units in Hispanic communities, and the evangelizing and missionary vision of Hispanic leaders and workers. These and other secondary causes are responsible for the existence of the Hispanic Mennonite Church of North America. Each state and each congregation has its own peculiar reasons for its existence, growth, and development. Each congregation has its own unique story and as such should be told.

Texas

Texas is the true cradle of the Mennonite work among Hispanics. Although we agree, as has already been indicated, that the formal beginning of the church was in 1932 in Chicago, the seed to develop Mennonite work among Spanish-speaking people had already germinated some sixteen years before when in 1916 Simón Del Bosque participated in a congregation in Tuleta, Texas.

Mennonites, who since the first immigrations had settled in the northern states, began to move toward south Texas during the first decade of this century and settled in the area near Normanna, some sixty miles from Corpus Christi. In 1905 Peter Unzicker, a minister from Illinois, bought a large piece of land on which he founded the town of Tuleta. Already by 1906 there were six Mennonite families living in that sector and in January 1907, a congregation of twenty-one members was organized. The congregation prospered numerically and by 1913 had 104 members. But this progress was stopped by the conditions of the First World War (1914-18) and by a serious drought that hit the region in 1917. For these reasons many families had to move north and find refuge in the states of Indiana, Ohio, Kansas,

Illinois, and Missouri. In spite of these hardships several families remained in the area.

Due to the participation of Del Bosque in the congregation of Tuleta, D. H. Bender and S. E. Allgyer, representatives of the Mennonite Board of Missions and Charities, made an investigative trip to south Texas during February and March of 1920, beginning in Brownsville, a city on the Mexican border. But nothing further came of this investigation except the confirmation that there was a mission "gold mine" on the U.S.-Mexican border.

In 1927 the Canadian, E. S. Hallman, moved to Falfurrias, one hundred miles south of Tuleta, in search of a climate more agreeable with his precarious physical health. Hallman joined with H. Frank Reist and together they carried the responsibility of the preaching in Tuleta. During this period the church began to push ahead again and by 1932 it had three dozen members.

In this same era of the late twenties, specifically 1929, Amos A. Schertz moved with his family to Falfurrias, where his son Arthur and his daughter-in-law Dorothy began to lead Sunday schools among the Hispanics. (They did the same in the border town of La Gloria.) The majority of these Spanish speakers were Mexicans who had crossed the border following the harvests on the farms. Many returned to their country, but others settled in the communities near the border.

It was not until the middle of the thirties that Tuleta became the central base for reaching the Spanish-speaking community of the southern region. In 1935 T. K. Hershey[1], a missionary on furlough from Argentina, was convinced that a mission work should be established among the Spanish speakers of south Texas. The Mennonite Board of Missions in its annual meeting of that year passed a resolution that favored the establishment of a mission in that part of the country and named Hershey and William G. Detweiler to investigate. Hershey and Detweiler studied the situation and told about the area's magnificent opportunities for evangelism.

Hershey arrived in 1937 to begin the work. David Alwine, from Pennsylvania, also arrived to collaborate in the project. Alwine, who was self-supporting, had his own business in Pettus, near Tuleta, and worked with Hispanics in the town of Helena.

They began to hold services each Sunday afternoon in the Hispanic schools of Normanna. Simón Del Bosque, the first Spanish-speaking convert and who more than two decades before had become a member of the church in Tuleta, would now be the key instrument in reaching the Hispanics. Del Bosque translated the Sunday services, made contacts, and served as a bridge between the missionaries and the Hispanic people. In this way the first Hispanic Mennonite in North America played an important part in the development of the work in Texas.

On January 2, 1938, the first baptism took place in Normanna, three miles from Tuleta, where seven were baptized and twelve received as members. In December of the same year the Mennonite Mission of Normanna was organized. The establishment of this mission was due to the work of leaders such as E. S. Hallman, H. Frank Reist, Amsa H. Kauffman, and David Alwine.

Hallmans left Tuleta in 1950 and moved to Akron, Pennsylvania, where they lived the last years of their lives. From this time the story of migration toward the north was repeated and by 1957 the congregation had almost disappeared. Beginning in this era the nucleus of the mission of south Texas would be more toward the south and the west, where the present congregations are located today: Mathis, Alice, and Corpus Christi.

Iglesia Menonita del Calvario, Mathis
(Calvary Mennonite Church)

When Hershey arrived in Texas in the thirties he had an itinerant ministry in mind, in which the workers would preach in different locations of the southern region without becoming established in any one place. This idea was based on the migrant character of the local population. Thus, during the first decade services were held in Helena, Normanna, Mathis, Benavides, Premont, and Falfurrias.

But practice contradicted the theory. They soon realized that in spite of the temporary employment of the people, they needed to become established among them and live with those whom they wished to serve and help them in their social and economic problems in addition to their spiritual ones. This meant that they would have to have a stable center in some part of the region. But where? Mathis, called the vegetable center of south Texas, was selected because a good number of the people interested in the gospel lived there.

Thus the Calvary Mennonite Church was organized in 1944 under the leadership of Amsa H. Kauffman. A house was purchased that would serve as a place for meeting as well as a home for the mission workers. The church grew rapidly and at the end of a year had some fifty members.

When the Kauffmans left in 1946, several workers provided interim leadership. Among these were Frank Byler and William Lauver, both related to the mission work in Argentina. In this same year the congregation joined the South Central Mennonite Conference.

In 1948 Eldo J. Miller assumed leadership of the work. Services were held in his home with the attendance occasionally reaching 63 persons. They then constructed a small church building. When Miller left, T. K. Hershey again appeared, this time as a retired missionary, and in 1950 provided leadership for a short time.

As near as can be determined, after this period of many changes in leadership, the congregation entered an era of stable leadership and solid growth. Numerical growth was accompanied by growth in program and community service. This began in 1951 with the naming of Weldon Martin as the leader of the work in Mathis.

During this era Elvin Snyder, a missionary from Argentina, arrived in south Texas to assume the responsibility of professor of Spanish in the high school of the city of Yorktown. Snyder traveled with his family every Sunday to Mathis, some 80 miles away, to help in the services. Supposing that Snyder was well acquainted with the situation, the Mennonite Board of Missions asked him to make recommendations for the improvement of the work in Mathis. He pointed out various basic needs of the Hispanic community in addition to the message of salvation: the establishment of a kindergarten to teach English to the preschool children and prepare them to enter first grade, maternity and medical facilities for the Hispanic women, the construction of housing that would help stabilize families, and recreational activities for the Hispanic children.

In 1955 an annex was constructed for educational activities and later, in 1956, an auditorium was built with accommodations for up to 250 persons. The building was dedicated on August 10. This was the first time that the growing congregation had an adequate place for its work. This large and attractive building is located at 719 West San Patricio Avenue.

The Mathis congregation longed to go beyond the borders of its own town and so in January 1956 services were begun in the town of Alice. Paul Conrad, who had originally arrived to work in Voluntary Service, and the pastor, Weldon Martin, began to hold services on Sunday afternoons and, later, on Sunday mornings.

In 1962 the church, with its earnest desire to serve the community, helped the hundreds of persons affected by the devastation of hurricane Carla. Paul Conrad, who since the decade of the fifties had been working among the Hispanic people of south Texas, was ordained to the ministry in 1962. The congregation now had a flourishing membership of 130. The growth was so great that the pastor needed an assistant and so Samuel Hernández was licensed for a year for that function.

During this time the Voluntary Service units played an invaluable role in the development of the work in Mathis. In addition to work in the kindergarten, in the block factory, and in the medical services, the Voluntary Service workers offered industrial arts training, crafts and sewing, supervised recreational activities, and taught Sunday school and summer Bible school. Later, units were established in Alice, Premont, Robstown, Corpus Christi, and Brownsville. From the arrival of the first volunteers in 1952 until the present, more than two hundred have served in the Hispanic Mennonite work in south Texas and made major contributions to its development.

During the decade of the 60s many young people of Mathis left to seek education in the colleges of the denomination: Lupe De León, Lupe García, Irma Guzmán, Samuel Hernández, and Verardo González, among others. This tendency was rare for those times, since few Hispanics attended any university and fewer yet the Mennonite educational institutions. Today we see a boom in educational studies with dozens of Hispanics students in Mennonite colleges. Other young people of Mathis have followed the movement and two members of that congregation have just graduated from Goshen College: Fidencia Flores and Magdaleno Hernández.

When Paul Conrad left, the congregation obtained its first Hispanic pastor, Atanacio Paiz, who was licensed in August 1970. Before this, Samuel Hernández had been assistant pastor and Adolfo Saldivar, interim pastor.

In the first years of the decade of the 70s employment was limited in the city and surrounding areas. This forced many families to move resulting in a decline in church membership. By 1971 the membership had dropped to 117. However, by 1975, according to the *Directory of the National Council, 1982-84,* the membership reached 151, which makes the church of Mathis the congregation with the largest membership of all the Hispanic Mennonite congregations of North America.

In 1972 Weldon Martin, who had been pastor during the years of maximum size, returned to take up the reins. In 1974 the church invited Armando Calderón, who was pastoring the Mennonite Church of Defiance, Ohio, to assume leadership in the Mathis church. Calderón pastored the church until 1981. Then Guillermo Tijerina, pastor of the church in Archbold, Ohio, took charge of the congregation on an interim basis for one year. On his leaving the church was without a pastor. As this is being written Ramiro Hernández, a recent graduate of the Hispanic Ministries Department of Goshen College, was to become the pastor beginning in May 1983.

Iglesia Menonita de Alice, Alice
(The Alice Mennonite Church)

The Alice Mennonite Church began in 1956 as a result of the missionary outreach of the Mathis congregation. Weldon Martin and other leaders of his congregation held the first worship service in this city on January 1, 1956. During the first month services were held Sunday afternoons, but within a month Paul Conrad and Sam Swartz, who lived in Premont, began to hold services Sunday mornings.

During August 1958 the work received a good push: the Voluntary Service unit from Mathis came to help develop a summer Bible school. Many children attended and several parents became interested in the work. In this same year Silvestre V. Zapata began to lead regular Bible studies on Wednesday evenings and Sunday mornings. Also, in November of that same year, two Voluntary Service couples arrived who were to play a principal role in the development of the work: Joseph and Norma Hostetler, and Allen and Bernelle Kanagy.

They began to hold Sunday evening services in 1959 and Zapata was licensed to serve in the ministry. During the same year a building was found at 1413 Consuelo Street, which would be the first home of the Alice Mennonite Church. Later an annex was added that could accommodate some 80 persons.

When Zapata moved to Premont in 1960 to help in the work there, Allen Kanagy was named to provide leadership for the Alice congregation. In addition, Richard Musser and his family moved to Alice to assist in the program.

The first persons were baptized in March 1962. Those baptized were four women, all grandmothers: Manuela Guzmán, Hipólita Guerra, Francisca Treviño, and María Luera. In addition to this outstanding event, before the end of the year another of equal importance occurred: Raúl Tadeo, who since 1959 had been helping with the work in Alice, was installed as the first full-time pastor. Tadeo had studied two years at Eastern Mennonite College.

In 1967 Tadeo resigned to continue his studies at Goshen Biblical Seminary. For this reason Joseph Hostetler was named as interim pastor, a position he held until his resignation in 1970. However, it was not until July 1972 that the congregation had another pastor when Ruperto Guedea was named to occupy the position. Guedea, who was from the Lawndale Mennonite Church and had studied at Hesston College, had been a congregational leader in Denver, Colorado, and pastor of the Mennonite Church in Defiance, Ohio. Guedea occupied this position until July 1974 when he began to work in the Congregational Health Insurance Plan and the South Texas Mennonite Church Council. In that year Israel Lozano was named as a part-time pastor. There was a brief time from May to July, 1976, in which the church was closed.

Because of this situation Guillermo Tijerina was asked to come to open and reorganize the church. It was decided to form a ministerial team of three persons, each to work in a different area of the congregation. In June 1977, a team was named composed of Daniel Bueno, responsible for worship; Ruperto Guedea, pastoral work, and Antero Rodríguez, youth ministry. At the end of the first year, Bueno resigned and Daniel Miller took his place. This team continued until 1981 when Guedea left to study in the Hispanic Ministries Department of Goshen College and Rodríguez left for Eastern Mennonite Seminary in Harrisonburg, Virginia.

In this same year, 1981, they obtained the services of a new pastor, Eduardo Monge, who occupies that position until the present. Monge, a native of Costa Rica where he attended the Mennonite Church, is a graduate of the Río Grande Bible Institute.

Since its beginning, the Alice Mennonite Church has remained active in the planning and development of various programs: Mennonite Youth Fellowship, a kindergarten, a women's organization, and clubs for boys and girls.

One of the excellent contributions of the church to the community is the Rancho Alegre Juvenile Center. This center provides a program of recreational and educational activities as well as Bible studies for the youth of the community. Voluntary Service has supplied personnel so that the congregation could operate this center. Rancho Alegre serves as a living testimony to the community and fills a vacuum in the lives of those young people.

Alice plays an important role in the history of the denomination, since it was from here that the concern came that ultimately resulted in a principal modification in the insurance programs of the Mennonite Church. In a meeting held in Alice it was emphatically pointed out that the Mennonite Mutual Aid insurance premiums were too high for members with few economic resources to pay. This denominational agency studied the situation and as a result they created the Congregational Health Insurance Plan, CHIP, which would help these needy members. Later, other Hispanic Mennonite congregations became a part of the program.

In general the format of the worship services is bilingual. On Sunday mornings there is first a sermon in English and then in Spanish. This is to be expected since about three fourths of the group are Spanish-speaking. According to the *Directory of the National Council,* 1982-84, the Alice Mennonite Church presently has 40 members.

Príncipe de Paz, Corpus Christi
(Prince of Peace)

Traditionally, the Hispanic Mennonite churches of south Texas have been established in small towns but the church in Corpus Christi is an exception. This important port city on the coastline of the Gulf of Mexico has a population of over two hundred thousand of which fifty percent are Spanish speaking.

The beginnings of the Prince of Peace Mennonite Church go back to 1956 when the Mennonite Board of Missions sent Don and Marilyn Brenneman to work among the Hispanic people of Corpus Christi. Don felt at home in the Spanish language since he had grown up in Argentina. The first services were held in the Brenneman home located at 4422 Kilgore Street. Only two persons came to the first service, the Brennemans, themselves. Later they began to meet in the rented cafeterias of the Prescott and Chula Vista School. In 1958 the Brennemans left Corpus Christi to assume the pastorate of the Lawndale Mennonite Church.

In August 1958, Weldon and Lorene Martin, who had pastored the church in Mathis, replaced the Brennemans. The congregation was organized in April 1962. The group began to grow and decided to buy a plot of land for the construction of a building. In 1962 this initiative led to the purchase of six lots on Horne Street for their new church building. Already in August of that year they held the first services in the new facilities which were dedicated on October 29.

In March 1965, after seven years of service, Weldon Martin left the congregation at Corpus Christi. He was replaced by Elvin Snyder who served from 1965 to 1968. William Hallman, another ex-missionary from Argentina, gave leadership for two years, 1968 to 1970. When Hallman left, Paul Conrad, who had also served in Mathis, took the reins of the congregation in September 1970. Conrad became the pastor with the longest tenure in this congregation since he did not leave until a decade later in June 1980. When Conrad left, the church remained without a pastor for a time until Jacobo Tijerina, who had worked with Home Missions and studied at Goshen College, accepted pastoral responsibilities in the summer of 1981.

The Voluntary Service unit, begun in 1959, played an important part in the development of the work. The volunteers collaborated in a countless number of projects such as clubs for boys and girls, a kindergarten, and summer Bible school.

The church is composed of families with names such as Reyes,

González, and Martínez. Leaders such as Lupe García, Guadalupe Longoria, and Raúl Hernández have been key persons in the development of the Hispanic Mennonite work in Corpus Christi.

This congregation, which in the past had as many as 60 members, now has only 25. However, between the wind and the waves, it continues to be a faithful witness to the Spanish-speaking community of that well-known Texas city.

Iglesia Menonita Evangélica, Taft
(Mennonite Evangelical Church)

The congregation at Taft was begun by Nelson and Lois Kreider, who had been in Voluntary Service in Mathis during the decade of the fifties. The Kreiders, who had worked as counselors in the public school system, were immediately aware of the great need for a work in Taft due to the large number of persons who attended no church. From that moment they were alert to ways of reaching persons of that community. They obtained the use of a small church building belonging to the Methodist Church where they could hold their services. At the same time Ruth Brubaker and Savilla Ebersole decided to cooperate with the Kreiders in the development of the work.

On August 2, 1970, the first Sunday school was held with a total of twenty-five present. The following day, August 3, hurricane Celia hit the region and destroyed part of the church building. The tragedy turned out to be a blessing because they were able to not only repair the building but to construct several additional rooms.

From this moment due to the hard work of leaders such as Elías Casas, the congregation grew and attained an attendance of 65. The time had come to obtain a full-time pastor. The Kreiders could work with the children and the youth, but they needed someone to work with the adults who spoke Spanish and desired a Hispanic pastor. They secured the services of a young Mexican, Fernando Pérez, but almost immediately he had to leave due to problems with his immigration documents.

While this was happening, God was preparing a young man from the Mathis Mennonite Church, Gilberto Pérez, to meet the needs of the congregation in Taft. Pérez had been studying two years in the Río Grande Bible Institute and now was ready to put his shoulder to the wheel. The congregation extended an invitation and on July 2, 1972, he was licensed and installed as pastor. Pérez left at the end of 1973 and the congregation remained without a pastor until 1975 when they obtained the services of Joe Hernández for one year. Later, Ben Blanchard, from the congregation in Brownsville, served as pastor for one year in the late seventies. When he left one year later the congregation was once again, and still is, without a pastor.

The lack of a pastor, the migration of many persons, a case similar to Premont, and other factors have contributed to the fact that presently only 15 persons attend the services. However, the work continues through the efforts of lay persons such as Virginia Sifuentes.

Iglesia Menonita del Cordero, Brownsville
(Mennonite Church of the Lamb)

The work in this town on the Mexico-Texas border was begun by Conrado Hinojosa.[2] During the decade of the seventies Hinojosa lived in Archbold, Ohio, where he was employed at Sauder's Woodworking Plant. In 1964 he was converted and baptized in the Hispanic Mennonite Church in Archbold. After his conversion, Hinojosa dreamed of returning to minister to the people of Brownsville, where he had grown up since coming from Mexico at the age of three. He continued working at Sauder's, but several years later he developed rheumatoid arthritis, which confirmed his decision to return.

Thus it was that in December 1969, Conrado, Esther, his wife, and their five children returned to Brownsville. Hinojosa's fervent desire to work among the people of his district continued and, recognizing his need for theological training, he enrolled in the Río Grande Bible Institute in January 1970. He also began to visit homes and talk of the Christ whom he had learned to know and love. Soon he began to hold services in one of the homes and the attendance began to increase.

Due to the growth of the group they began to look for a larger place in which to meet. They found an old abandoned house at 3404 27th Street. They carried out mountains of garbage, installed windows and doors, and cleaned and painted. After three months of hard work the house was ready for use in February 1971. In spite of the fact that they had no benches or electric light, six or seven persons attended the first services. Soon the house began to fill with people and they were able to build benches and make the necessary deposit for electric service. The pulpit, which they still lacked, was donated by a Methodist church in the community.

On April 20, 1972, the first eight persons were baptized. Included in this group were Conrado's brother and father. The baptism was in charge of Guillermo Tijerina, pastor of the Good Shepherd Mennonite Church of Archbold, Ohio. In this same year they requested affiliation with the South Central Mennonite Conference and Hinojosa was licensed. In addition, they organized a women's group and a church council. At this point in its development, the congregation wanted a church building and Simon Gingerich, associate secretary of Home Missions, visited Brownsville in December 1972, to find a place where a new building could be constructed. A five-acre lot was purchased in 1973 for the construction of the longed-for church building. Construction was begun January 15, 1974, with the help of Mennonites from the area as well as from Ohio and Indiana. The result of this cooperative effort was a beautiful brick Spanish-style building located at 1033 North Minnesota Avenue which was given the name Iglesia Menonita del Cordero (Mennonite Church of the Lamb). The building was finished but it still lacked benches. These were donated by Sauder's Woodworking Plant, the company where Hinojosa had worked some years before. The building was dedicated May 5, 1974. Guillermo Tijerina, at that time pastor of the Temple of the Lord, brought the message for this important and significant occasion. In 1976 a Sunday school annex was constructed.

The present membership of the congregation is ninety-eight. Worship services are held solely in Spanish and with the exception of the adult classes, Sunday school is only in English.

Voluntary Service units have played an important role in the development of this congregation. At the present time the unit, in cooperation with the congregation, is involved in the construction of homes for low-income families. This serves as a witness to the Brownsville community and has helped to reach some of the persons that now attend the church. In addition, the congregation administers a day-care center that provides services to many community families.

The Brownsville Hispanic Mennonite congregation has not

limited itself to serving only its immediate community but has spread the gospel and begun congregations in the Mexican cities of Matamoros, just across the border, and Celaya, two hours distant. The work in Matamoros, called the New Jerusalem Mennonite Church, was begun in 1974 and today has an attendance of thirty persons. Homero Ruiz served as the pastor in the beginning followed by David Ramírez who has carried out the pastoral duties the past few years. The work in Celaya was begun in 1977 when Victor Castellanos, who had attended the church of Brownsville for three years, decided to return to his hometown and witness for his Savior and Lord. Today the congregation has a membership of 27 and a Sunday morning attendance of 38.

Iglesia Menonita El Mesías, Robstown
(Messiah Mennonite Church)

Although Voluntary Service workers had been in the city of Robstown since 1962, the congregation was not formally organized until the decade of the seventies. The church had a presence from the beginning in the family of James Miller, in the reconstruction work done by members of Mennonite Disaster Service during the hurricane in 1971, and in the Sunday schools sponsored by members of Voluntary Service.

In spite of these contacts and expressions of service, the work did not move forward until the fall of 1973, when Gilberto Pérez, the pastor of the congregation in Taft, and Francisco Rodríguez, a member of the church in Mathis, began to hold evangelistic meetings twice a week. In December 1973, Pérez presented a report to the South Texas Mennonite Church Council in which he pointed out that there was a good number of persons in Robstown who were responding favorably to the visitation program. The council decided officially to begin the work in that city.

During the later part of the month of December 1973, Pérez and his family moved to Robstown and held the first service at 1019 Indiana Street. Later they moved to 1037 Ohio Street where the group began to take shape and grow. The group grew to the point that by the spring of 1978 the inadequacies of that location and the need for new facilities were obvious.

On March 8, 1978, the congregation, with financial assistance from the Mennonite Board of Missions, purchased a lot at 526 Industrial Street. It was then that they changed the name of the congregation from Mennonite Mission to Iglesia Menonita El Mesías (Messiah Mennonite Church). In April of the same year the Home Missions division donated the building that once held the already extinct congregation of Premont and it was moved to Robstown.

In August 1978, the remodeling and enlarging of the building was begun with the assistance of the Brownsville Voluntary Service group. Members of other congregations in the area also helped in the project. Finally, after months of work, the repairs were completed and the building was used for the first time on December 22, 1978. It was dedicated on January 21, 1979, with a beautiful service in which the following significant words were read. 'For the blessing of the family and the home, for the instruction and the teaching of the children, for the inspiration of the youth and the guidance of all, to help the needy, to promote the brotherhood, and extend the kingdom of God to all the world."

To these definite and significant objectives the congregation firmly responded, "We dedicate this temple."

This congregation holds all of its services in Spanish. The program of the church includes weekly activities such as Bible studies in homes and prayer services in the church. In addition the youth and the women have organized themselves to develop their own activities and as a group assist in the development of the work.

The Messiah Mennonite Church presently has more than 40 members and a Sunday school attendance of more than 80.

The South Texas Mennonite Church Council

As the number of congregations grew there was a parallel effort to find ways to unify the work. Already by the end of the seventies there was talk of the formation of a council. But many questions and uncertainties concerning the real function of such an organization kept the idea from being developed. Many thought that this would be a body that would make all the decisions and that, therefore, it would take away the autonomy of the local congregations. In 1970 another effort began to form an organization of the south Texas churches. This time the feelings were more positive and the atmosphere more tranquil. Thus, after long discussions they decided to work toward the formation of a council emphasizing that its primary function would be to advise, and this, clearly, in aspects that affect the regional programs. Finally, Lupe De León was elected interim president to organize another regional meeting for the purpose of planning the steps to take in the formation of a council.

From this point they proceeded to ask the congregations to send interim delegates. The leaders coordinated the activity and the selected delegates met January 24, 1971, in Robstown and selected a committee of five members to write a constitution that would delineate the policies to be followed by the council. This constitutional committee was composed of Jesús Navarro (Premont), Paul Conrad (Corpus Christi), Guadalupe Longoria (Alice), Lloyd Miller (Robstown), and Manuela García (Premont). After several months of work the committee completed a constitution which would be presented in March of that same year in Mathis. In this meeting the constitution was accepted.

On March 2, 1971, the official delegates of all the Mennonite churches of the region plus one delegate from a Voluntary Service unit met in Corpus Christi and adopted South Texas Mennonite Church Council or STMCC as the official name of the organization. They also elected the first administrative committee composed of Jesús Navarro, president; Israel Lozano, vice-president; Nelson Kreider, secretary; and Daniel Miller, treasurer. The purposes of the council were described as follows: direct and implement items pertinent to the regional programs of the church; direct the Voluntary Service projects that are not under the administration of a specific congregation; promote the different service agencies of the denomination (Mennonite Disaster Service, Mennonite Board of Missions, etc.); promote a vehicle by which the congregations will receive council in congregational affairs; and promote and supervise the extension program in south Texas.

From that memorable date in May 1971, the council has been carrying out with precision the functions that were specified. This demonstration of solidarity, communication, understanding, and cooperation would serve as a model and inspiration to the total Hispanic Mennonite Church.[3]

Ohio

Iglesia Menonita del Buen Pastor, Archbold
(Good Shepherd Mennonite Church)

Beginning in 1940 the northeast region of Ohio began to attract a large number of Hispanics who came looking for farm work, the majority from Texas and Mexico. They came with their families each summer to pick fruits and vegetables and as time passed, more and more were attracted by the employment opportunities in the new factories. Slowly they began to establish themselves in the region, obtaining more permanent employment. As always occurs in the immigration process there were problems of culture and language. The language barrier caused many frustrations that were reflected in their spiritual lives, since it made it difficult for them to attend and participate freely in English-speaking congregations.

Several persons in the Mennonite churches of the region began to become interested in the spiritual and social condition of the Hispanics. The figure of William Flory stands out among these interested persons. This brother, together with a local committee, began to look for ways to help the Hispanic population. They searched diligently for someone who could speak Spanish. The group communicated with David Alwine, who had been one of the pioneers in the Hispanic Mennonite work in south Texas. Since Alwine had lived in the Hispanic community for almost four years he seemed to be the ideal person to provide leadership. Alwine was attracted by the challenge and consented to come to work in Ohio among the Hispanics. He and his family arrived in the area in August 1940. Immediately, he began to hold services in Spanish on Sunday afternoons in the Central Mennonite Church of Archbold, located some thirty miles west of Toledo and about ten miles south of the Michigan border.

In the winter of that same year, Alwine organized a school to teach Spanish to those who were interested in learning that language. This was for the purpose of relating to the Hispanics since there were few Mennonites in the region who could speak Spanish. In the beginning there was great interest. Twenty-eight began the course. However, by the end of the course only four remained. One of these finalists was Flory who continued to work diligently with Alwine in the Hispanic work.

During the summer of 1941 they began to hold services in other locations where Hispanic families were living: in a school two miles east of Tedrow and in a building near Delta. By the end of that summer six persons had made professions of faith. Of these six, three were baptized in March 1942. In addition to these activities and accomplishments, during the summers of 1942 and 1943 they held Sunday schools and Sunday services in the Lockport Mennonite Church.

Unfortunately, in the summer of 1943, Alwine left behind his responsibilities in the Hispanic congregation to respond to the call of a congregation in Johnstown, Pennsylvania. Although he was ordained on July 25, 1943, he led his last service among the Hispanics in Ohio on August 29.

When Alwine left, Flory was selected to continue the work. Flory gave his all to the enterprise and continued to hold services in the different localities and in the homes of interested persons. This brother did not limit his work to the propagation of the gospel but also put into practice the beautiful gift of unselfish service.

During the decade of the fifties services were held Sunday afternoons and evenings in a school located one mile north of Archbold. The group began to grow and would soon need a church building in which to meet. In 1959 a member of the Archbold congregation donated a plot of ground and the Good Shepherd Mennonite Church was constructed. The name of the church, based on John 10:11, proclaimed the yearning to reach the community and the desire to serve. The new church building was inaugurated in March 1960, and formally dedicated in October of that year.

The attendance was not very stable since many were migrant workers. In addition, Catholic opposition was firmly entrenched. In spite of this and other inconveniences, Flory continued to provide leadership to the congregation until his death on April 7, 1963.

When Flory died the congregation was left without a pastor. Thus they asked Guillermo Tijerina, who had been a member of the congregation and was now serving as pastor in Defiance, to come and provide leadership for his home congregation. Tijerina accepted the call and pastored both congregations for three months until the congregation in Defiance obtained another pastor. He began working full time in the ministry on April 5, 1965, and on July 25 was ordained in the Good Shepherd Mennonite Church.

During the pastorate of Tijerina the group developed and became a stable and mature congregation. In 1969 he resigned his pastoral position but continued to attend the services. He was replaced by E. Bullers, who remained for two years, 1971-73. When Bullers left, Tijerina resumed the pastoral responsibilities. Later, he went to Texas to assist a congregation of that region that had requested his help and Raymundo Gómez was invited as pastor. Gómez remained until June 1978, when Tijerina returned. Tijerina has served as pastor until the present. In the early eighties he left for several months to help the congregation in Mathis which was without a pastor. During his absence other leaders of Good Shepherd assumed responsibilities, especially the lay leader David Tijerina.

Their services are simple and informal, totally in Spanish. The youth use English Sunday school materials and the adults Spanish.

The Good Shepherd Mennonite Church presently has a membership of 39 persons and a Sunday attendance of 50 to 60. Recently the congregation has experienced both numerical and spiritual growth.

Primera Iglesia Menonita, Defiance
(First Mennonite Church of Defiance)

While the attraction for the Hispanics in Archbold was agricultural, in Defiance, a city fifteen miles southeast of Archbold, the attraction was industrial. General Motors built a plant in Defiance in 1948 that provided a large number and variety of jobs. Among the persons attracted by these employment opportunities were many Hispanics, especially Mexicans and Puerto Ricans. In addition, other industries appeared in the area stimulating the growth of the Hispanic community. Thus by the fifties, the sizable Hispanic community of Defiance presented a challenge, which the Mennonite Church of Ohio had already accepted in Archbold.

Among the members of the Hispanic church of Archbold were two young Puerto Ricans, Alfredo Bonilla and Rubén Fuentes, who felt the need to take the gospel to the newly established Hispanic community of Defiance. Thus, in 1956, these young men in collaboration with their pastor, William Flory, began to visit homes and to encourage members of their congregation to collaborate in the Hispanic work in Defiance. Slowly the work began to flourish and the pioneers realized that they were going to need assistance from the Mennonite Board of Missions. The Board of Missions agreed to help and Board leaders met with representatives from the Mennonite churches in the region. In this meeting a committee was formed consisting of a delegate from each congregation for the purpose of obtaining a place where the Defiance Hispanic group could meet for their services.

In 1957 they obtained the services of Victor Ovando, a native of Nicaragua, as their pastor. After five years Ovando accepted the call to serve in a Hispanic work in Chicago and Ruperto Guedea, a member of Lawndale Mennonite Church, took his place for ten months. When Guedea left, the congregation was without a pastor but continued to meet.

In an attempt to find a solution for the problem of leadership, representatives of all of the congregations of the region met with Nelson Kauffman of Home Missions. They asked that one of the local congregations accept the responsibility to continue the work. None of the congregations accepted and so they presented the same request to the Good Shepherd Mennonite Church. This congregation accepted the request with the plan that their leaders and pastor would take turns each Sunday as ministers in the home congregation. Clearly, this arrangement was intended to function until such a time as they could find permanent leadership.

William Flory, Marciano Serna, Gene Richer, and Guillermo Tijerina provided the leadership that the work required. This arrangement continued for six months, until one of the leaders of the group felt the call to serve fully in the Hispanic community of Defiance. Guillermo Tijerina made the decision to accept the ministerial work in November 1962, and on January 20, 1963, he was licensed in the Good Shepherd Mennonite Church.

Unfortunately, three months after Tijerina had begun his pastoral work in Defiance, William Flory died. As a result Tijerina worked in both congregations for some three months. Finally, in August 1963, they obtained the services of Armando Calderón, who had been converted in Defiance, and Tijerina returned to serve in the work in Archbold. Calderón was licensed to the ministry of the congregation in Defiance July 25, 1965, and occupied this position until August 1974, when he left to pastor the congregation of Mathis, Texas.

When Calderón left, Weldon Martin, who had served in the Hispanic congregations in south Texas, served as pastor for almost one year. Martin moved to Goshen, Indiana, and the congregation that had passed through a time of transition and adjustments, now, in addition, needed a new pastor.

During this time, Benjamín Vázquez, who was from a Pentecostal background, began to visit the church and was accepted as pastor. This period became one of more changes and adjustments, since Vázquez brought with him his Pentecostal characteristics and emphasized and promoted them in the Mennonite church. This caused many frustrations and disagreements among the members. They held a meeting of the congregation and the Mennonite Board of Missions and decided that it would be advisable to change pastors. This decision produced a division in the congregation in August 1978. The original members remained while the new members decided to establish their own church.

The congregation was without a pastor and so David del Río, one of the leaders, accepted the responsibilities of leadership until a pastor could be found. This congregation, passing through its first problem of this magnitude, remained strong and in prayer. Thus in August 1978, they obtained the services of Aureliano Vázquez, who had studied in the Río Grande Bible Institute and had been a member of the Hispanic church in Moline. He began his work as pastor September 13 of that year. Now the congregation began a period of pastoral stability since Vázquez continues in that position to the present.

In addition to his pastorate, Vázquez ministers in the Hispanic community of the region through radio. His first radio program was aired Sunday, July 22, 1979. The fifteen-minute program transmitted over WOMW is called "I Was Found."

The church building located at 1129 Ayersville Avenue has a very good relationship with the other Hispanic churches in the community. They often meet together to celebrate special occasions such as anniversaries.

The worship services are informal with the singing of many

choruses. In the Sunday school they use both English and Spanish materials. The women hold a central place in this congregation. They lead the worship, teach, and on occasion, preach. In addition they have a sewing circle that sends its finished products to places of need.

The First Mennonite Church of Defiance has a membership of 40 and a Sunday morning attendance of 70 to 80.

Primera Iglesia Menonita, Fremont
(First Mennonite Church of Fremont)

In March 1980, Israel Bolaños, a native of El Salvador, began the work in the city of Fremont, some thirty miles southeast of Toledo. After having received approval from the Evangelism Commission of the Ohio Conference, Bolaños made a preliminary investigation of statistical data on the Hispanic population of Fremont.

Following this initial step he proceeded to make contact with the Hispanic community through visits to Hispanic businesses such as stores, bakeries, and producers of tortillas. Having made these initial contacts he extended invitations to the services held in the Bolaños home at 536 Union Place. In this way he made himself known, introduced and presented the gospel, and described the denomination and the purpose of his presence in the city.

This process of visitation took approximately six months. During this period he learned to know the other pastors of the area and asked to use the fellowship hall of the Trinity United Methodist Church. They rented the room and in September 1980 began to hold worship services from 3:00-5:00 on Sunday afternoons. Later, they were able to arrange for the use of the sanctuary, the services were changed to one o'clock, and they began to hold prayer meetings on Wednesday evenings.

The services began with from five to ten persons but the attendance increased until by September 1982 they had an average attendance of 50. During this time ten persons were received as charter members and eight were baptized. In February 1983, two more were baptized bringing the membership to twenty.

Presently the Sunday school is composed of three classes: adults, primary, and preschool. A church council has been organized and church officials elected. The number of services has increased: they have Sunday morning worship, Sunday evening service, Bible study on Wednesday, and Bible studies in different homes throughout the rest of the week according to the needs.

Bolaños and his congregation are not content with just reaching the Hispanic community of Fremont but use the radio to reach more souls. During the summer of 1982 they began the program, "Momentos de Meditación" (Moments of Meditation) which is transmitted each Saturday evening at 8:00 by WMEX, 100.9 FM. The fifteen-minute program reaches the surrounding Hispanic populated areas. This fruitful ministry is supported by voluntary contributions.

Pennsylvania

The Hispanic Mennonite work in Pennsylvania began in 1950. It was in this era that T. K. Hershey, who had been a missionary in Argentina for some thirty years and had helped start the Hispanic work in Texas, arrived in Pennsylvania and began to establish contacts with the Hispanics of the southeastern region of this beautiful state. These Hispanics were primarily Puerto Ricans that came to work in the apple orchards and in the tomato and potato fields during the summer and who returned to the Island for the winter.

In spite of his advanced age (he was already 70 years old) Hershey sensed a tremendous opportunity to present the message of salvation to these migrant people. He began to visit the farms where the migrants worked and offer weekly services during the months of July, August, and September. These services were held in four different Mennonite churches in the area of Lancaster but not simultaneously. Hershey preached in one congregation on Saturday evening and in the other three on Sunday morning, afternoon, and evening, respectively.

The property owners cooperated with Hershey's work and encouraged the workers to attend the services. As a result of these combined efforts, the attendance at some of these meetings reached two hundred persons. Hershey was very enthusiastic with the work and planned a united meeting of all the Hispanics in the area. This activity produced considerable interest and hundreds of persons attended and took advantage of the opportunity to hear a message in their own language and share with other Hispanics of the area.

Unfortunately, after several years, Hershey had to leave the work because of declining health. Then the work, which was now under the Eastern Mennonite Board, utilized the services of various persons who had worked as missionaries in Spanish-speaking countries. Among these leaders were John Litwiller (Chile), Addona Nissley (Puerto Rico), Isaac Frederick (Honduras), Jacob Rutt (Argentina), and James Martin (Uruguay). It was at this moment in history, 1954, that the Eastern Mennonite Board, seeing the need for permanent workers, asked William G. Lauver to direct the Hispanic work. He had been a missionary in Argentina for many years and had served in the beginning of the work in Texas. This event marked the beginning of stable leadership that was to produce the formal beginning of the churches.

Iglesia Menonita Hispana, New Holland
(Hispanic Mennonite Church of New Holland)

In 1953 the decision was made to hold permanent services in New Holland, a town located some thirty miles west of Philadelphia. This action was taken due to the fact that a group of Hispanics had settled permanently in New Holland to work at Victor Weaver's, a chicken processing plant that provided work all year. Thus when Lauver arrived in New Holland in the summer of 1954 a group was already meeting on Sunday mornings on the second floor of the English-speaking Mennonite Church.

Lauver began to develop the work and by 1956 the first group of believers was baptized. The congregation grew and prospered. In this same year they moved to a building at 213 Main Street on the west side of town. This building was soon too small so they moved to a church building two miles south of the city. For health reasons Lauver had to leave the work in July 1969, after fifteen years of leadership and hard work. George Miller then took the reins of the congregation and served until 1975.

The members and leaders of the congregation realized that the church building was too far from New Holland so they began to look for a location in the city. About this time the English-speaking congregation had constructed a new church building and decided to sell the old one, located at 24 Roberts Avenue, to the Hispanic group. The congregation decided that they wanted a Hispanic pastor and invited

Rafael Ramos, a native of Honduras who had lived in the community since 1972, to accept the position. Ramos assumed his responsibilities in the summer of 1975 and served until his resignation seven years later, due to his obligations as general secretary of the Hispanic Council of Region V. José M. Ortiz then provided leadership for a short time but the church is now without a pastor.

The congregation presently has a membership of 29 and a Sunday school attendance of 40.

Iglesia Menonita del Buen Pastor, Lancaster
(Good Shepherd Mennonite Church of Lancaster)

When William G. Lauver came to Pennsylvania his work was not limited to the group in New Holland. He also began to hold services in the homes of believers on Friday evenings in the nearby city of Lancaster where a sizable group of Hispanics lived. In spite of this and other previous efforts, the work did not become stable until Elmer Weaver, who had worked in Puerto Rico, assumed leadership. Weaver was licensed in 1963 and remained at the head of the congregation until 1969. May 25 of that same year Artemio de Jesús, who had come from Puerto Rico in 1961 and had been converted in that same congregation in 1964, was installed as pastor. The congregation, which met in a building in the center of the city, began to grow and soon the place was too small. They began to collect funds and look for a place to construct a church building. In 1970 the dream was realized and a beautiful building was constructed at 645 Harrison Street. The new facility was dedicated December 19, 1970.

In 1971 de Jesús felt called to begin a new work in New Jersey and resigned his pastoral responsibilities. On Sunday, September 12, 1971, José A. Santiago, who had just come from Puerto Rico, was installed as pastor of the congregation. During the period of Santiago's pastorate there was a great interest in mission work and members of the congregation went out to start other churches both in the United States and overseas. Work was begun in Philadelphia (Eugenio Matos), New Jersey (Artemio de Jesús), Florida (Enrique Ayala and Isidoro Sáez), Washington, D.C. (Caonabo Reyes), Guatemala (Juan Vega), Puerto Rico (Héctor Caballero), and the Dominican Republic (Artemio de Jesús).

In addition to the missionary work in other U.S. cities and other countries, the members felt the burning desire to minister to the immediate community. Members such as Tibulsio Bodón and María Acosta dedicated themselves to work with children and their attendance greatly increased. This growth led to the purchase of a bus for transportation and the construction of an annex, which was dedicated April 27, 1975.

In 1975 Santiago resigned his pastoral position to assume the responsibilities of general secretary of the Council of Hispanic Mennonite Churches. César Segura, a native of the Dominican Republic, took his place and was installed September 21, 1975. Segura left in 1976 and was replaced temporarily by Artemio de Jesús. In June 1977, they obtained the services of Rosemberg Rojas who occupied the position until August 1982, when he left to serve in the recently opened work in Wilmington, Delaware. He was followed in the pastorate by José A. Santiago, who had just returned from Venezuela where he had served in the beginning of the Mennonite work in that South American country. Santiago was installed September 19, 1982.

This congregation now has a membership of 40 and a Sunday attendance of 60. But the contribution of this congregation cannot be measured solely by these numbers. It has produced an outstanding number of leaders that have known how to put their hand to the plow and contribute significantly to the growth of the Hispanic Mennonite work in both North and Latin America.

Luz Verdadera, Reading
(True Light)

In June 1960, José González, Gabriel Matos, and Ramón Ocasio, three members of the New Holland congregation, felt the desire to begin to minister in Reading, some 20 miles northeast of New Holland. Every Sunday afternoon these men visited the home of Gamaliel Colón, who had opened the doors of his home for worship services. Shortly thereafter Colón's three daughters accepted the Lord and interest began to spread. The group grew to such an extent that they had to look for a larger place in which to meet and rented a room that had once been a barbershop, for twenty-five dollars a month. Immediately, with the collaboration of the members, they fixed up their new chapel located at 324 6th Street and on May 20, 1962, they celebrated their first baptism.

In 1963, due to problems with the sanitary facilities of the building, they moved to the English-speaking Mennonite church on North 7th Street. There they held their services on Sunday afternoons since the English group used the facilities in the morning. Soon, with financial help from the Eastern Mennonite Board they purchased a church building located at 1003 Franklin Street and inaugurated the new facilities on Saturday, October 17, 1964.

From the time the congregation was first organized until the decade of the eighties, González served as pastor. He was followed by Candelario Matos, who is the present pastor. Matos was ordained to the ministry on February 25, 1983, in a service in which José A. Santiago was in charge of the ordination and José M. Ortiz preached the message.

The congregation presently has a group of young people called "The True Light Youth Group," which is dedicated to visit other congregations to present programs. In addition to this ministry the congregation has explored a new field in the Hispanic Mennonite Church: television programming. Their program is televised through Berks Cable on channel 3 of ACTV each Thursday at 10:30 in the evening and at noon on Saturday.

This congregation presently has a membership of 58 and a Sunday school attendance of 94.

Arca de Salvación, Philadelphia
(Ark of Salvation)

During the decade of the sixties many Hispanics moved to Philadelphia and a large number settled in the area surrounding the Norris Square Mennonite Church at 2147 Howard Street on the north side of the city. This congregation was interested in the spiritual and physical well-being of the Hispanics and thought that the best way to promote this would be to establish a Hispanic department. The Eastern Mennonite Board was also interested in the project and so it was presented to the Council of Hispanic Mennonite Churches. After several meetings and visits to the area they decided to begin a work there.

On January 9, 1971, José A. Santiago began to make contacts in the large Hispanic community in the city. In June, Eugenio Matos and Candelario Matos began to help in the work. Later Eugenio decided to dedicate himself fully to the work and on June 13, 1971, he was installed as assistant pastor of the Norris Square Mennonite Church in charge of the Hispanic department and sharing the ministerial work with James Lehman, pastor of the English department. In the summer of 1972, the first baptism was held with ten persons being baptized in Black Rock Lake near Lancaster. Later the leaders of the Hispanic group realized that it would be more convenient to have a totally Hispanic independent congregation so after consulting with the English-speaking leadership, they made the necessary arrangements.

After several years Eugenio Matos left for Trenton, New Jersey, to serve in the Hispanic work in that city. Matos was followed by Benjamín Pérez and Isidoro Sáez who occupied the leadership for relatively short periods. It was Arcadio Tolentino, who then assumed the pastorate in 1977 and continues to serve.

In the summer of 1982, this congregation opened an extension in North Philadelphia lead by Herminio Acevedo. The ministry of this congregation includes services in the city jail.

This congregation presently has the largest membership of all of the churches in Pennsylvania (65) and also the largest Sunday school attendance (161).

Estrella de la Mañana, Pottstown
(Morning Star)

This congregation was begun in 1974 as a mission of the Reading congregation. In the beginning the work was pastored by Gabriel Matos. He was followed in the pastorate by Benjamín Pérez and Wilfredo Rodríguez. The present pastor is Artemio de Jesús who was installed in the early part of 1981. The congregation emphasizes missionary work and has used its offerings to help in the translation of the New Testament into the Triqui dialect of Mexico and to put a new roof on a church building in the Dominican Republic.

The congregation which meets at 515 Walnut Street has a membership of 25 and an average attendance of 50.

Kennett Square, Kennett Square

In August 1977, José González and Rosemberg Rojas began to visit and hand out Bibles and tracts to the many Hispanics that worked in the mushroom fields of the little town of Kennett Square. Later José Polanco was named officially to work in this area and began in December 1978. When Polanco died in 1980, Ray González assumed the pastoral responsibilities until 1982 when he resigned. After González left, the small group was without a leader for a time until Benjamín Pérez began to hold services in homes in February 1983.

Jesucristo es la Respuesta, Harrisburg
(Jesus Christ is the Answer)

It was in July 1980, that Benjamín Pérez*began the Hispanic Mennonite work in the city of Harrisburg. Pérez directed the group that developed until September 1982, when he left to begin the work in West Chester, Pennsylvania. Pérez was replaced by Ramón Vargas, who had been the assistant pastor for some time. Vargas was installed and licensed October 31, 1982.

West Chester, West Chester

Benjamín Pérez, who pastored the Hispanic church of Harrisburg, moved to West Chester in September 1982 for the purpose of opening a work in that city where there were so many Hispanics. Upon his arrival he began to organize a group that today numbers some 40 persons and meets Tuesday, Friday, and Sunday in the Presbyterian Church of that city.

Iglesia Menonita Hispana, York
(Hispanic Mennonite Church of York)

In 1982 Magín Pérez began to explore the city of York for the establishment of a Hispanic work. He held Bible studies in different homes and the group began to grow. Later, the English-speaking Mennonite church, Tidings of Peace, let them use their facilities for their worship services. On December 11, 1982, an inauguration service was held in which Pérez was commissioned as pastor of the congregation.

Council of Hispanic Mennonite Churches

Already by the end of the sixties a concern was in the air to unite the churches and establish an organization that could direct, administer, and provide a corporate vision. On April 11, 1970, all the pastors and Hispanic leaders of Pennsylvania met for the first time in the conference room of the Eastern Mennonite Board for the purpose of creating an instrument to direct their collective work. At that time there were only three Hispanic Mennonite congregations: New Holland, Lancaster, and Reading.

It was not, however, until May 30 of that year that the Council of Hispanic Mennonite Churches was officially organized. The following board of directors was named: José A. Santiago, president; Artemio de Jesús, vice-president; José González, secretary; Gabriel Matos. treasurer; and Héctor Caballero and George Miller, members at large. Their first annual assembly was held May 29, 1971, in the New Holland Hispanic Mennonite Church. Since that moment they have held thirteen assemblies with themes such as "The Church; Its Nature and Mission," "The Living Church," "The Church Versus the World," and "Extending the Kingdom of Christ."

Presently there are twelve congregations in the council, including those in Delaware and New Jersey. An executive secretary provides the administrative leadership for the organization. Rafael Ramos, who was installed January 24, 1981, is the present executive secretary. Ramos was preceded by José A. Santiago and César Segura. The present board of directors is composed of: José A. Santiago, president; Benjamín Pérez, vice-president; Artemio de Jesús, secretary; Héctor Moreno, treasurer; and Eugenio Matos and Arcadio Tolentino, members at large. Other persons that have served as president of the board of directors are: Artemio de Jesús, César Segura, and Rosemberg Rojas.

In a meeting held January 10, 1981, in Trenton, New Jersey, the council drew up several challenging goals for the decade of the eighties: (1) to work for the extension of the church by taking the good news to all the surrounding Hispanic communities; (2) to build and strengthen the congregations now in existence and those to be formed; (3) to assist the pastors in their theological education, Christian stewardship and ministerial ethics, administration, and congregational responsibilities; and (4) to improve the relationship between the council and the conferences, and work together with the total church.

The case of the Hispanic Mennonites of Pennsylvania is interesting because, in addition to being the state with the largest number of congregations (9), they have excelled in organization and ardent desire to spread the Word of God. The council and the congregations have not only worked for the evangelization of the immediate area, their "Jerusalem," but have gone also to "Judea" and have established congregations in Washington, D.C., Florida, New Jersey, and New York. They have also reached "Samaria" in Puerto Rico, the Dominican Republic, Guatemala, and Venezuela. This work is unique in the Hispanic Mennonite church and extraordinary because Hispanics have been thought of as receivers and not as missionaries on foreign soil.

In addition to these significant achievements, the council has created a theological training organization with the title Mennonite Theological Institute, begun August 5, 1971, when José A. Santiago, James Hess, George Miller, and James Sauder met in the New Holland church to plan for a theological training center. Today the institute has 13 teachers and 38 students distributed among four centers (Vineland, New Jersey; Philadelphia, Pennsylvania; Trenton, New Jersey; and New Holland, Pennsylvania). The vision of this institute is to help each congregation train its lay and pastoral leadership to carry out the Great Commission of making disciples, to generate good programs, and to establish new works. The leadership of the Institute, Benjamín Pérez, president, and José M. Ortiz, director, has planned several future projects: go to the congregations that request it; offer credit for the studies; begin to form libraries stocked with magazines, books, and reference materials; and hold monthly meetings of the faculty and students.[4]

In addition, the council, recognizing that the youth play an important part in the life of the church believes that a person should be named to dedicate specific time to this ministry. David Acosta, an active young man from Lancaster, was named youth secretary in 1982. Due to this impetus the youth that belong to these churches are well organized and very active.

New York

The immigration of hundreds of thousands of Puerto Ricans to New York is one of the most interesting contemporary social phenomena. Although there were already Puerto Rican immigrants in the nineteenth century, it was not until after the Second World War that the immigration from the Island reached its peak. Before this mass exodus, in which more than half a million Puerto Ricans left the Island, there were already 60,000 in New York. In 1974, according to the U.S. census figures, the Puerto Rican population in the U.S. reached 1.5 million of which a conservative estimate would place at least one million in the New York metropolitan area.

The congregations in New York City thus began as a result of the massive postwar exodus from the Island. Some of these Islanders had a Mennonite background which provided the groundwork for the beginning of the Hispanic work in the great metropolis.

Primera Iglesia Evangélica Menonita, Brooklyn, New York
(First Evangelical Mennonite Church)

Gladys Widmer, a missionary from Iowa who had worked in Puerto Rico for several years, came to the U.S. for vacation and personal reasons. Widmer took advantage of a New York trip to visit several persons that she had known in her missionary work in the beginning of the Coamo Mennonite Church from 1954 to 1957. Among these persons was the family of Angel and Aquilina Torres, since the mother of Aquilina was a member of the Mennonite Church of Coamo. Widmer visited the family January 19, 1957, and Aquilina expressed her spiritual concern and her decision to accept the Lord as her Savior. These concerns where not impulsive since they had been accumulating for some time due to a variety of experiences: her eldest daughter, Ana Hilda, who had been converted in Puerto Rico while living with her maternal grandparents, came to New York with Christ in her heart and the Bible in her suitcase; and her mother, Librada, had always spoken of Christ. Now the seeds began to bear fruit.

Thus Widmer realized that there were many members of the Mennonite church of Puerto Rico now living in that community in the great New York metropolis and decided to begin meeting in several homes that same week for prayer services. Aquilina asked to be baptized and Widmer went to the Board of Missions for counsel. They sent John Driver the following Sunday, January 29, 1957, and in the living room of their apartment in the presence of family and friends, she was baptized.

Widmer remained in the city for longer than she had planned in order to help the small group move ahead until they could obtain permanent leadership. The attendance increased creating the need for a larger permanent place in which to meet. On September 29 of that same year they rented a place for forty dollars per month at 8 Suydam Avenue that had been a laundry. Fixing up the place was hard work. Since the Chinese owner had died suddenly, the building was full of trash. Each family brought paint from their home to paint the building. The paint was all mixed together producing a sky blue color. Once the place was prepared they held an evangelistic campaign October 13-29. Victor Ovando, at that time pastor of a Mennonite church in Ohio, was the evangelist. Widmer described this first stage in the development of the new congregation in the following way:

> "Hitherto has the Lord helped us." 1 Sam. 7:12 was written on the blackboard at 8 Suydam (our church location) last Wednesday evening. The first anniversary of this beginning fellowship was celebrated at that time. It has been an inspiration to watch the growing group, continually leading out in the work, sometimes against very trying circumstances. First they met in their homes; since October they have been renting a building on 8 Suydam for services. You would not recognize the place as being the same one when the first night of cleaning began! The second floor is not yet finished but, as we say, "poco a poco" (little by little). This floor is now being used for Sunday school classes and Saturday youth and children's activities. Two baptisms were held during the year, one in January and another on New Year's Eve. Several others are desiring to take this step soon. Remember them in prayer as well as the entire fellowship and including those of their families and friends whom they are endeavoring to lead to Christ these days.[5]

During this beginning period there were a number of workers who collaborated: Samuel Miller, who had been a missionary in Argentina and now lived in Harrisonburg, Virginia; John Smucker, who had begun what is now known as the Mennonite House of Friendship; and John Litwiller, who was studying in Hartford, Connecticut.

There were also several workers in New York who helped with the Sunday school classes: Sara Ann Classen, Helen Rufenacht, Rhoda Ebersole, and others. During the summer several brothers such as Fernando Cains and Angel Luis Miranda came from Puerto Rico.

Following the example of Aquilina, who is still a strong pillar in the Brooklyn congregation, several other persons were baptized and became leaders of the group: Aurelio Rodríquez, who made his decision October 8, 1957, and was baptized December 31 of that same year, and Lucia López, who came to faith in Christ October 18, 1957, and was baptized February 16, 1958.

The congregation celebrated its first anniversary January 29, 1958. Serafín Rivera, a native of Puerto Rico who lived in the Bronx, was the preacher for that occasion.

The congregation now had a large group and a place to meet but was still without a pastor. In March 1958, Juan Isaís, Manhattan agent for the Editorial Caribe of Costa Rica, suggested that Guillermo Torres could help them. Torres had come from Puerto Rico where he had been a pastor in the Christian Missionary Alliance Church. He preached in the congregation for the first time March 16, 1958, and a short time later, November 30, 1959, was installed as part-time pastor of the Brooklyn church. The installation was held in the White Reformed Church of Bushwick Avenue with sermons by John Litwiller, directed to the pastor, and Rogelio Archilla, directed to the congregation. Paul Lauver presided and Samuel Miller presented the Bible. In 1960, with financial assistance from the conference, Torres began to work full time in the congregation.

In 1959 the congregation became affiliated with the Convention of Mennonite Churches of Puerto Rico. Since Puerto Rico was so far away, this affiliation was changed in 1969 from the Puerto Rican Convention to the Ohio and Eastern Conference of the Mennonite Church in order to better meet the needs of the congregation. Later the congregation became part of the Atlantic Coast Conference of the Mennonite Church and of the Council of Mennonite Churches of New York City.

From 8 Suydam Avenue the congregation moved to a rented facility at 1035 DeKalb. When this was taken over by the city for an urbanization project they had to rent another place at 1050 Broadway on the third floor next to the elevated train tracks on which a train passed every ten minutes. Since the building did not meet safety regulations the fire department ordered them to vacate. A short time later the building burned. From there they moved to a more adequate location at 12 Jefferson. During this time the congregation had been saving money and searching for a building which they could purchase. There was a synagogue for sale on 23 Sumner but when they heard the asking price of $40,000 they decided to look for a place that was financially within their reach. A year later they learned that the price was now $30,000 so with financial help from the Mennonite Board of Missions they purchased and repaired it. At last the dream of having their own building became a reality. The building was dedicated to the Lord with a superb service September 18, 1966.

After almost two decades of service, Torres resigned his pastoral functions in 1976 due to failing health. Aurelio Rodríquez, who had been baptized on the first New Year's Eve of the congregation's existence, took the reins of the congregation. Several years later they obtained for a short time the pastoral services of Pedro Oliva. Finding themselves without a pastor, several members led by Reinaldo Pacheco took the responsibility of providing the necessary leadership. In 1982, they obtained the part-time services of Bolivar Colberg, of Puerto Rico, who was then installed in 1983.

Presently the Brooklyn congregation, the pillar of the Hispanic Mennonite churches of the city and prototype of strength and perseverance, has a membership of 32.

Bronx Spanish, Bronx, New York
A large number of Hispanic Mennonites from the congregations in Puerto Rico and from Brooklyn had lived in the Bronx for several years. Although there were three English-speaking Mennonite congregations in this borough which offered Sunday school classes in Spanish, the Hispanics wanted their own congregation. That which the English congregations offered was not sufficient. They needed a more nourishing experience.

The family of Angel and Celia Torres is a good example. This couple, which had accepted Christ in 1958 shortly before arriving in New York, was baptized in the First Mennonite Church of Brooklyn

April 20, 1959. But the physical condition of Celia and the distance made regular attendance difficult. They had to travel for more than an hour and a half by subway to reach the Brooklyn church. Again the question was raised, "Why can't we have a Spanish-speaking congregation in the Bronx?"

Finally, the Brooklyn congregation decided to respond to the request. Guillermo Torres and Gladys Widmer began to hold a series of services on Friday evenings in different homes in the community for the purpose of feeling out the situation and search for the will of the Lord. The first service was held October 23, 1964, in the home of Rosa and Miguel Santiago with ten persons present. Later, services were held in other homes with an average attendance of sixteen.

After this beautiful beginning there was no doubt that they should continue to meet regularly. With this in mind they looked for a more spacious place to meet. Angel Torres obtained permission to rent the facilities of the Melrose Reformed Church at 748 Elton Avenue at the corner of 156th Street. The group could meet Friday evenings for a payment of fifty dollars per month rent. The first service was held December 4, 1964. By December 20 they were holding Sunday services at 2:30 p.m. and by November 1965, they added Wednesday evening prayer services.

In the beginning they did not have a pastor. Laymen from Brooklyn such as Obed Maldonado, Reinaldo Pacheco, Aurelio Rodríquez, and others brought the Sunday afternoon messages. In addition the Mennonite Board of Missions suggested that Samuel Miller and Ross Goldfus help whenever possible.

September 21, 1965, eleven months after their first service, the group officially organized as a congregation with ten baptized active members: Serafín and Zenaida Rivera, Angel and Celia Torres, Luis and Sonya Santiago, Blanca Marrero, Paula Rivera, Tomasita Castillo and Felícita Hernández. They elected the following church council: Guillermo Torres, president; Angel Torres, secretary; Serafín Rivera, treasurer; and Blanca Marrero and Sonya Santiago, members at large.

In January 1966, the Reformed Church asked them to leave because they were planning to use the building more frequently and they wanted to begin their own services in Spanish. On February 16 they rented the building of a Holiness Church that was located several blocks from the previous location for sixty dollars per month. But problems with the heating system and scheduling difficulties sent them searching for a place they could rent as their own.

In April 1966 they rented a place at 3153 Third Avenue for 125 dollars per month. This building was right next to the elevated train tracks. Samuel Miller, who led the first service there April 14, 1966, described the event in the following way:

> I was with them for the Friday evening service in their new location at Third and Brook Avenues. Due to some misunderstanding the light company had not connected the lights so we met without light. I could see my Bible by the light of the street and they sang by memory. There was a good crowd there considering the circumstances. . . . The place is central, near the people and elevated train stop as well as main bus stops. The train passing of course is noisy but it doesn't pass so often Sundays. I am frankly enthusiastic about the Spanish church in the Bronx. I know the enthusiasm is with something new on their part and there will be problems but there have been plenty of those already. The fact of whole families attending is very encouraging.[6]

In spite of the fact that the congregation continued to move forward with giant steps they still lacked stable pastoral leadership. In January, Ronald Collins, who was teaching at the Christopher Dock Mennonite High School in Pennsylvania, was asked by Nelson Kauffman to travel regularly to the Bronx to lend his services. In February, Collins began to travel to the Bronx every fifteen days to preach on Sunday afternoons. April 6 the members decided unanimously to ask him to be their pastor. Collins obtained a position teaching physics in the Voorhees Technical Institute, a junior college in Manhattan, and on July 4 he and his family moved to the Bronx. In September he was licensed as part-time pastor of the congregation in a service in which Lester Hershey brought the message. On July 6, 1969, the Puerto Rican Mennonite Convention ordained Collins as pastor.

By the spring of 1967, the Third Avenue location was too small for the needs of the growing group. They decided to purchase a four-story building at 160 Street and Elton Avenue, three blocks from the Third Avenue building. On September 1, 1967, with financial aid from the Mennonite Board of Missions they purchased the building for $21,000. The dedication of the building was held October 29,

1967, in a service in which Nelson Litwiller brought the message.

In addition to obtaining a pastor and buying their own building, the congregation had other accomplishments during this period: an increase in attendance and membership, the first summer Bible school, and the first Voluntary Service couple.

In the summer of 1970, Collins tendered his resignation to be effective July 1, 1971. Marcos Chico, an ex-drug addict from Puerto Rico who had grown up in New York, was called to be their pastor. Chico left a short time later and was replaced by José Feliz, who served as pastor from April 6, 1973, until September 1, 1980.

In 1978, because of the deteriorating conditions of the area, the congregation sold the building. Presently they meet under the leadership of Angel Ortiz in the facilities of the English-speaking Burnside Mennonite Church and hold their services at 2:30 Sunday afternoons and some evenings during the week.

According to the *Directory of the National Council, 1982-84*, the Bronx Spanish Mennonite Church has a present membership of 16.

Templo el Peregrino, Manhattan, New York
(Pilgrim Temple)

Mario de Orive came to the United States from Spain April 2, 1952, and after five months began to hold services and Bible studies with Spanish-speaking persons. De Orive purchased Bibles and hymnals in Spanish with the limited financial resources that he received from his work at the newspaper,*Ecos de Nueva York (Echos from New York)*. The group, which had developed voluntarily and independently, was incorporated in New York City in May 1956. In the beginning they met in the church buildings of various denominations, plus the 23rd Street WMCA and a motel room on 82nd Street. Finally, they obtained a more permanent meeting place in the French-speaking Pilgrim Temple, at 126 West 16st Street.

The first contacts between de Orive and his group and the Mennonite Church were begun in October 1958. Juan Isaís told him about the congregation in Brooklyn and de Orive became interested and paid them a visit. From this moment a relationship was established that culminated in the affiliation of the group with the Mennonite Church in the early seventies.

De Orive died in September 1975 and the attendance of the congregation, that had reached 33 members, decreased considerably. Presently the congregation with about ten members is under the leadership of Aurelio Rodríquez and holds its services Sunday afternoons at 2:00 p.m.

Iglesia Unida de Avivamiento, Brooklyn, New York
(United Church of Revival)

The United Church of Revival, pastored by the Dominican, César Segura, had existed as an independent congregation for several years. In September 1973 it requested affiliation with the Council of Hispanic Mennonite Churches of Pennsylvania. On Sunday, April 7, 1974, the congregation was publicly received as part of the Lancaster Mennonite Conference and pastor Segura was officially installed. Paul Landis, bishop of the Hispanic congregations; José González, president of the Hispanic Council; and José A. Santiago, executive secretary, officiated. In 1975, Pastor Mateo, also from the Dominican Republic, became pastor of the congregation, taking the place of Segura who had been transferred to pastor the Church of the Good Shepherd in Lancaster, Pennsylvania.

The congregation had to vacate its facilities at 1147 DeKalb Avenue due to its deterioration, limited space, and lack of heat and met for several months in the pastor's home. This increased the pressure to buy a meeting place and on May 17, 1976, they purchased a building at 169 Knickerbocker Avenue. The new facilities were inaugurated July 3, 1977.

In 1979 for several reasons, especially the distance, the congregation became part of the New York district. In 1981, Pastor Mateo was named superintendent of the council of New York, so the congregation named Nicolás Angustia as their pastor. The present membership of the congregation is 35.

Morris Heights, Bronx, New York

On February 15, 1977, the Morris Heights congregation became affiliated with the Council of Mennonite Churches in New York City. The majority of this group including its pastor, Juan Suero, and his wife were members of the Bronx Spanish Mennonite Church. They meet in a small rented room at 117 East 175th Street.

According to the New York administrative reports, this group is outstanding for its work with children. In a short period of time they gained more than thirty. The present membership of the congregation is 17.

Efesios, Manhattan, New York
(Ephesians)

This congregation became affiliated with the Council of Mennonite Churches in New York City the same time as Morris Heights, February 15, 1977. It meets at 243 West 15th Street and is pastored by Salomón Arias.

This small group with a membership of 25 appears to be dynamic and worthy of emulation. The report to the VI Convention of the National Council indicates this.

> This small group has prospered in every sense of the word. Several new members have been added and several were baptized. They continue to search for a temple to purchase. Although the membership does not reach thirty, it is the richest congregation in the Mennonite Council in New York City. This is not because the members are rich but because they are faithful. They have accumulated nearly forty thousand dollars with help from no one and without sales of any kind. This amount has been collected only from tithes and offerings.[7]

Bethel Spanish, Amsterdam

Between 1970 and 1971 César Segura was preaching on several occasions in the city of Amsterdam, where several persons accepted Christ as Savior. Later, between 1975 and 1976 José A. Santiago and Rogelio Feliciano made periodic trips to that city. These first contacts led to the decision to begin work there. Thus on July 23, 1977, a special inaugural service was held with the installation of Rogelio Feliciano as pastor. The moderator of this special occasion was César Segura with José González bringing the principle message. Chester Wenger, of Eastern Mennonite Board, José A. Santiago, and several members of the Lancaster congregation were also present.

At first the congregation used the facilities of the Second Presbyterian Church but recently they have purchased their own building on

Principal Street. In the beginning the congregation was affiliated with the Lancaster Conference but in 1979 they became part of the New York district. The congregation has a membership of 28.

Iglesia Cristiana Valle de Jesús, Brooklyn, New York
(Valley of Jesus Christian Church)

Beginning independently, this congregation became part of the Mennonite Church in 1982. It is unique in the history of the Hispanic Mennonite Church in North America in that it is led by a woman, Mercedes González. The group has a membership of 21.

Council of Mennonite Churches in New York City

All of the Hispanic Mennonite churches in the New York City area belong to this organization founded in 1980. The dominance of Hispanics is obvious: of the 14 member congregations, 8 are Spanish-speaking, and of the 366 members, 184 are of the same group.

Iowa

Segunda Iglesia Menonita, Davenport
(Second Mennonite Church)

Gladys Widmer, who was primarily responsible for the beginnings of the work in New York, was also the initiator of the Hispanic Mennonite work in her home state of Iowa. In 1956 Widmer arrived in Iowa from Puerto Rico, where she was a missionary, to help her parents through a time of illness. To her surprise she found Spanish-speaking persons in Muscatine and Davenport, cities near her home in Wayland.

In the winter of 1957, Edith Roth, a teacher from Wayland who taught classes in the area, introduced Widmer to two Hispanic families, one from Puerto Rico and the other from Colombia. She took advantage of this opportunity to learn to know other families in the community that showed interest in the gospel. Later, she accompanied a group from Wayland which traveled to Davenport to hold services in English in the home of a Hamilton family. A lady who did not understand English came to these services and asked that Widmer translate. Then Widmer learned that William G. Lauver, who had served in Argentina and was presently living in Davenport with some of his children, had also made some initial contacts.

In April 1960, during Easter week, Widmer took José M. Ortiz and Luis Vargas, who were then students at Hesston College, to minister in the area. They held a service in the home of the Zapata family and several members expressed interest. Although Widmer visited the homes whenever she was in Iowa, there was no continuity since no one in the Mennonite churches of the area spoke Spanish.

It was not until 1962 that contacts were reestablished when José M. Ortiz, who had now graduated from Goshen College, returned during July and August to work with the Spanish books of the library on wheels that the Iowa-Nebraska Mennonite Conference had donated for this purpose. During this time they began to hold regular services in Lend-a-Hand, a hotel for women. At times Lawndale Mennonite Church members such as Gutiérrez and Bustos would come but no one came on a regular basis.

Finally, Widmer directed the attention of the Iowa-Nebraska and Illinois conferences to the tremendous opportunity that they had to begin a work among the Hispanics of the community. In addition, other churches had expressed interest in beginning a work if the Mennonite Church did not do it. Thus the conferences decided to meet and consider the proposal. This took place on February 15, 1963, when representatives of both conferences and Nelson Kauffman of the Mennonite Board of Missions met in Davenport. The decision was affirmative: the Mennonite Church would support all aspects of the development of the work.

Since Mac and Mary Bustos had already visited and helped several times, it was thought that they were the ideal couple to provide leadership for the new work. They accepted the challenge and moved to the area on May 11, 1963. The first service was held on Mother's Day, but no mothers came. However, one man came with his two sons.

By June 30, 1963, they had an attendance of 42 persons at the services held at 3:00 p.m. Sunday afternoons. Later, during July, they decided to change the hour and meet at 10:00 a.m.

The congregation continued to grow and soon purchased a building at 700 East 6th Street which was dedicated May 3, 1964. In addition to the members, several ministers and visitors were present such as Melvin Hamilton, a member of the Mennonite Board of Missions; Norman Derstine, representative of the Illinois Conference; Leroy Miller, Eugene Gerber, and Harry Wenger, representatives from Iowa; and Mario Bustos, who brought the message. During the dedication service a couple was accepted into the membership of the newly formed congregation.

The first to attend the church services were the families of Teodulo Perales, Carmen Gaxiola, Pedro Sauceda, and Domingo Sauceda. The first persons baptized were Paula Sauceda and Desiderio González.

During this time Bustos began to hold worship services and Sunday school on Sunday afternoons in the nearby city of Muscatine. Later, in February 1969, Jorge Gómez, one of the leaders of the congregation, moved together with his family to Muscatine for the purpose of providing leadership for the small group that had formed.

On April 13, 1969, Mac Bustos was ordained to the ministry of the Hispanic Mennonite Church. The ordination was in charge of Dean Swartzendruber of Wellman, Iowa, and Rob Hubler, president of the Council of Mennonite Churches of the Quad Cities. Weldon Martin preached.

In that same year, 1969, the congregation experienced other significant events: they began to meet on Wednesdays; and the idea developed to purchase another church building in the nearby city of Moline.

However, it was 1970 that brought events of major importance for the congregation. On January 1, Bustos, who had been working in a tractor factory, began to work full time in the ministry. The dream to purchase a larger building in Moline became a reality. They purchased a building that had been a Catholic church located at 613 3rd Street for $32,000. The members painted and repaired and held their first service in the new location December 6, 1970. The building in Davenport was not sold but was used for the development of a variety of projects.

The Moline congregation marched forward steadily and in 1977 the Bustos family decided to return to the first building in Davenport and begin a new work. They were accompanied by his mother-in-law and Inocencio and Leticia Hernández. The congregation began to develop and before long the Bustos family left on sabbatical. When they returned in July 1981, they found that a series of problems had left the church almost empty. But now the new challenge began: to build a new congregation. This new development is described in *Ecos Menonitas*, April 1982, in an article, "A Trilingual Church":

> We began to pray and to search for the will of God. We had to start all over and we didn't know where to begin. After handing out tracts in the neighborhood and inviting the people to the services we decided to wait. We did not ask that the new people be Anglos or Hispanics, we only asked that people come to hear the message.
>
> On September 27, 1981, the congregation had special services. After about one hour, to the surprise of the small group of Hispanics present, a group of Cambodians entered. As they entered they greeted us with reverence since they knew neither English nor Spanish. Some of them embraced us. The next Sunday they brought their own interpreter. The services were held first in Spanish, then in English, and the translator translated into Cambodian. Today we have between 90 and 100 persons, primarily Cambodians. Whole families come from East Moline to listen and participate. One of the members of the congregation fixed up one of his vans so that he could bring some of them. Several have been baptized and others have made decisions for Christ....
>
> Today the congregation is a new congregation; we sing in Spanish, English, and Cambodian. We read the Bible in three languages, we comfort and help each other. We are a new trilingual community.[8]

Without a doubt the beautiful ministry of this trilingual congregation is unique in the history of the Hispanic Mennonite Church. This pioneer spirit of renewal is not new for the Davenport congregation since from its beginning it has been its distinguishing mark. This congregation, without doubt, is worthy of recognition, praise, and emulation in the Hispanic Mennonite family.

Iglesia Menonita de Muscatine, Muscatine
(Muscatine Mennonite Church)

The Muscatine Mennonite Church, as we have already mentioned, was an extension work of the Davenport congregation. Mac Bustos and Gladys Widmer were the ones who made the first contacts with the Hispanics of this city. The majority of them were Mexicans who came every summer following the tomato, melon, cucumber, corn, potato, and pumpkin harvests. Today, hundreds of families reside in the area and it is estimated that each year ten more families settle in Muscatine.

Because of this great opportunity, Bustos began to travel from Davenport to hold outdoor services. Later, they began to meet Sunday afternoons in the basement of a Baptist church. Thus the work continued, and in February 1969 Jorge Gómez moved to Muscatine.

Several years later Gómez moved to Jersey City, New Jersey, and the work was left without leadership. During this time Simón Rada moved to the area and took charge of the work. Rada, who had come to Iowa as a migrant in 1956 and later became a member of the Davenport Mennonite Church, returned after three years of study in the Río Grande Bible Institute.

On September 30, 1973, the first baptism was held with Rada assuming the pastoral responsibilities. Two persons were baptized and two were received into membership by confession of faith. These were: Arturo Rivera, Dora Rivera, and Efrén and Leonor Cardoza. That evening they celebrated communion with Dean Swartzendruber, Mac Bustos, and Héctor León officiating.

Rada, who had begun to work in Muscatine in 1971, was ordained to the ministry October 7, 1979. In this service Frank Brown, a missionary in Ecuador, preached the sermon.

The Muscatine congregation, following the example of its mother congregation, has begun to spread. In November 1981, two families of the congregation began to visit the nearby town of West Liberty, where a large number of Hispanics lived. It is possible that from this beginning will come the third Hispanic congregation in Iowa. Time will tell.

The congregation meets in its own building at 913 East 6th Street and has a membership of 38.

Oregon

Iglesia Menonita Pentecostés, Woodburn
(Pentecostal Mennonite Church)
In January 1964, Samuel Hernández left his native state of Texas

to visit his wife's parents in Oregon. Probably Hernández never imagined that he would come to live in that beautiful Western state for thirteen years, and even less, that he would be the one responsible for beginning the Oregon Hispanic Mennonite work. Hernández settled in Woodburn and immediately noticed that many Hispanics lived there with almost no Spanish churches in the community. The Baptist church which was beginning a work among the migrants was the only exception.

Hernández and his wife, Donna, began to attend the services in an Assemblies of God church where they learned to know several persons who were to play a key role in the development of the Hispanic work in Oregon: Magdaleno Martínez and H. C. Guzmán. Since they were looking for a place to worship in their own culture and language, they decided to attend the Spanish services that the above mentioned Baptist group was holding in Independence. But the distance and the environment made them want to hold their own worship services in Woodburn.

In the summer of 1964, Hernández began a radio program called "Vida y Luz" (Life and Light), which immediately helped him reach the many Hispanics living in Woodburn. These, in addition to the group he already knew, felt the need for a Hispanic church. Thus they began to meet in the home of Magdaleno Martínez just outside of town. Since the space in the house was limited, they met in the yard under an apple tree. This was really the beginning of the work at Woodburn.

Hernández and Martínez divided the work: the first preached and taught; the second visited and brought people to the worship services. This plan worked very well and the group began to grow. Seeing the need for more space, in 1965 they rented a veterans' hall. Sometimes the attendance there reached one hundred persons, but later, because of the intervention of another nearby denomination, the congregation was divided and the attendance decreased considerably.

By 1966, the congregation again needed their own place to worship. This was not because the group was so large but because the environment in the veterans' hall had become difficult. The dances that were held on Saturday evenings did not leave a favorable atmosphere for Sunday morning worship services. The Christian Church heard of the need of the Hispanic group and offered them their church building, since they were moving to a new one. Although the church building was large and ornate, the Christian Church was interested in the Hispanic work and sold it to them for only $6,000. In this way the congregation obtained its present building.

Hernández, who came from the Hispanic Mennonite church, did not at that time feel a part of the denomination in which he had grown up. Thus he chose the name Mexican Pentecostal Church for the congregation which denoted its independent status.

The small congregation possessed an enormous missionary spirit and attempted to establish congregations in Aloha in 1967 and in Independence in 1968. Neither attempt produced satisfactory results. The group did not become disillusioned but continued in their desire to reach people through another medium: television. In 1972 the congregation began producing a one half hour television program in Salem, which was transmitted every Sunday evening.

In 1972 the Pacific Coast Mennonite Conference together with Home Missions offered economic support to the Woodburn congregation so that Hernández could dedicate full time to the work. The receipt of financial assistance from these organizations raised the question of congregational affiliation. The lack of knowledge of the Mennonite Church on the part of the congregation and the great diversity of opinions lengthened the process considerably.

In 1977, Hernández accepted the pastorate of the Hispanic Mennonite Church in Goshen and Magdaleno Martínez remained in charge of the Woodburn congregation.

Finally, on January 27, 1980, the congregation became affiliated with the Mennonite Church. To commemorate the event a service was held in which Hernández, the founder of the work, preached the sermon and John Oyer, Conference Moderator, Harold Hochstetler, Conference Minister, and José M. Oritz, Associate General Secretary for Latin Concerns participated.

In February 1981, Víctor Vargas, from Costa Rica, took the place of Martínez who had left to work in another Hispanic work in Oregon.

Presently, the congregation of the Pentecostal Mennonite Church meets at 198 East Lincoln with a membership of 38.

Iglesia Jerusalén, Salem
(Jerusalem Church)

The television program which the Woodburn congregation began in 1972 helped open the doors to begin a work that was to produce a stable congregation. The congregation of Salem is pastored by José Campos and has a membership of 23.

Iglesia Menonita del Calvario, Hubbard
(Calvary Mennonite Church)

This group, pastored by Magdaleno Martínez has just begun and at the present time does not yet have any members in its official list.

Indiana
Iglesia del Buen Pastor, Goshen
(Church of the Good Shepherd)

Toward the end of the sixties there was a great concern for the well-being of Hispanics that came annually to the Elkhart-Goshen area in search of employment. The Mennonite Church, through students of Goshen College, members of College Mennonite Church, and others developed a series of sporadic programs of varied duration.

Mrs. Kathryn Troyer, who had lived in Puerto Rico for twenty-three years with her husband, Dr. George Troyer, thought that something was wrong when missionaries were sent overseas while the home mission was ignored. So it was that on October 12, 1969, Bible studies were begun at Pine Manor, a chicken-processing plant. She was determined to offer something that would be stable and continuous, since a short time before, the father of a large family who had been contacted previously by several lay leaders, took his own life. This concrete act called attention to the urgent need.

In November 1969, the Waterford Mennonite Church congregation provided assistance for Bible studies on Sunday afternoons in Bethany Christian High School. These Bible studies were led by Moses Beachy, who at that time was pastor of the East Goshen Mennonite Church. In the summer of 1970 the New Paris Methodist Church was rented for thirty dollars per month and on May 29 the first service was held in their new facility.

Amzie Yoder, who had been a missionary in Honduras and was

living in the Goshen area at that time, served as pastor for the first three months in the life of the New Paris congregation. Later, Teófilo Ponce, who had been a member of the Lawndale Mennonite Church and who had moved to Indiana in 1961, assumed leadership. Moses Beachy served as overseer.

During this same period the families of Roger Borneman and Warren Myers, who did not speak Spanish, transferred their membership from Waterford Mennonite Church to work with the children and youth who were more at home with English. Warren and his wife, Eva, continue to work in this important ministry.

On December 6, 1970, the Good Shepherd Mennonite Church became an official congregation when five persons were received by baptism, two by confession of faith, and thirteen by transfer. Among these first members were Leticia Ponce, María Luisa Dávila, Esperanza Dávila, Reina García, Rosa Gordillo, Inocencia Blanco, Kathryn Troyer, José Díaz, Roger and Irene Borneman, Moses Beachy, Warren and Eva Myers, and Diane, Christene, Manuel, Mary, and Teófilo Ponce.

In July 1971, the congregation obtained the pastoral services of Mario Bustos. During this era the attendance varied between 90 and 100 persons. The desire to have their own building led the congregation to purchase a spacious building that belonged to the Lutheran church for $25,000. The building was located at 523 South Sixth Street in the nearby town of Goshen. By July 1974, the congregation was enjoying its new facilities. The stained-glass window behind the pulpit was replaced by one donated by the Troyer family in memory of their late parents, who had played such an important part in the beginning of the congregation.

In July 1975, Mario Bustos died and the Indiana-Michigan Conference asked Teófilo Ponce to temporarily assume pastoral leadership. In December of that same year, Weldon Martin, who had been pastoring in Texas, was contacted and led the congregation until September 1977. Samuel Hernández, from Oregon, then took the reins of leadership and pastored until May 1979, when he entered Goshen College. The congregation was without a pastor for several months and was led by a team composed of Jacobo Tijerina, José M. Ortiz, and Lupe De León. Finally, on January 13, 1980, José Mojica was installed as pastor, a position he presently occupies.

This congregation is a unique case among the Hispanic Mennonite churches: it has some members who are permanent residents of the city and others who are associate members since they are students at Goshen College and live in the city for only part of the year. During the months when college classes are in session the attendance is high but during school vacations it is considerably lower. In addition, this factor produces a quite heterogeneous congregation. This fact makes the pastoral task and the adequate nurture of the congregation more difficult. But this congregational composition is also beneficial since a college student serves as assistant to the pastor. Due to this complexity, this congregation could be considered one of the most difficult and challenging.

The Church of the Good Shepherd, which in 1979 reached 67 members, today has only 41.

Iglesia Menonita Emanuel, Marion
(Emmanuel Mennonite Church)

Because of its interest in the Hispanics living in Indiana, the Mennonite Church through Home Missions director Simon Gingerich asked Teófilo Ponce to explore the southern and western areas of the state to determine the number of Hispanic churches in those areas. The investigation was to determine the following: denominations present, their work among Hispanics, the possibility of beginning a Hispanic work, and a recommendation on where to work.

Ponce, with his well-known pioneer and missionary spirit, began the assigned work. He investigated the situation on weekends for six months, distributed literature in the migrant camps during the day, and showed films during the evenings. This hard work led him to the conclusion that Marion, southeast of Goshen, was a good place to begin a work. Thus, in May 1977, the Mennonite Church, represented by Lupe De León and Galen Johns, of Home Missions and Indiana-Michigan Mennonite Conference, respectively, asked that he begin a work in that city. A church building was rented in June and the following month Ponce began to work full time as pastor of the newly begun work. The first worship service was held in July 1977, with eight persons present. They decided to name the congregation the

Emmanuel Mennonite Church. Already by October the attendance fluctuated between 30 and 40 persons.

Early in 1978 Ponce had some health problems and was replaced by Eduardo Acosta. During this time the congregation went through a series of difficulties that reduced the attendance considerably.

Acosta left and, on the request of the Indiana-Michigan Conference, Ponce returned in December 1979, and assumed leadership, or, more realistically, to begin the work again. They rented the church building of the Church of the Brethren for ten dollars per month. The attendance began to grow once again and on December 7, 1980, they officially became a congregation. Under Ponce's initiative the congregation has enjoyed the help of many students from Goshen College and other institutions of the Mennonite Church.

Toward the middle of 1981, Israel García assumed the pastoral responsibility replacing Ponce who served temporarily for more than a year. García was a product of the first harvests of the Church of the Good Shepherd of Goshen. He and his wife had been preparing for the ministry for several years and now returned to serve a sister congregation.

According to the *Mennonite Yearbook of 1983*, the Emmanuel Mennonite Church of Marion has a membership of 23.

Idaho
Misión Cristiana, Caldwell
(Christian Mission)

The Hispanic Mennonite work in Caldwell is closely tied to Rubén Esquivel. Esquivel, a young man from Mexico, arrived in Idaho as an immigrant. On one occasion he was put in jail due to an automobile accident in which he, together with some friends, all intoxicated, ran into a young man. In jail he accepted the Lord as his Savior through the ministry of a pastor named Reyes. Shortly thereafter, Esquivel entered the Evangelical Institute of La Puente where he studied for three years. On his return to the city he began to work among the Hispanics.

The initiative of Esquivel and his contacts resulted in the first service in a home on January 17, 1971. In March they moved to a vacant office building located in the center of the city. A little later they began to hold services for children during the week and the attendance increased considerably. In July they moved to the annex of a Baptist Church where they remained for several years with a Sunday worship attendance that oscillated between 20 and 40 people. On September 1, 1976, they purchased a building at 202 Kearney Street in Caldwell.

Between 1976 and 1979 the congregation began to decrease. Finally there were only three women and several children left. Later, some of the children moved to another community and the rest stopped attending.

However, the last Sunday of December 1979, one family returned and soon others followed. Today the Sunday attendance fluctuates between 30 and 50 persons.

On September 21, 1980, Rubén Esquivel, who had been with the congregation since its beginning, resigned the pastorate. Today the congregation is without a pastor but is receiving help from several sources: missionaries who have returned to the United States and one of the pastors of the Nampa Mennonite Church who helps the second Sunday of each month.

In addition, the congregation has several members who have provided leadership. Among these are Roy Rojas, deacon, and Mrs. R. E. Henry, who is the person responsible for the coordination of the congregational life.

This congregation, which began independently, joined the Mennonite Church in the summer of 1978.

Illinois
Iglesia Evangélica Menonita, Moline
(Evangelical Mennonite Church)

The Moline congregation has several distinctive characteristics: it is the only Hispanic Mennonite congregation in the state of Illinois located outside of the Chicago metropolitan area; it began with the move of the Davenport congregation to Moline; and, although it is in Illinois, it belongs to the Iowa-Nebraska Conference.

In 1970, as we have already stated, the Davenport congregation purchased a church building at 613 3rd Street and moved to Moline. They repaired what had once been a Roman Catholic church building and held their first worship service on December 6 of that same year.

The congregation has always been outstanding in its fervent desire to take the good news to the many migrants that come to the area each year. A credible example of this is the work carried out by Héctor and Febe León. This couple came to the area in June 1973 for the purpose of working with the Immigrant Evangelization Project. This summer project consisted of taking films, music and tracts to the migrant farm camps in Mendota, Muscatine, and Rock Island. Outdoor services were held with films shown after dark. When the Leóns left, others such as Pablo Gutiérrez, Emilio Villegas, and Aureliano Vázquez continued the work.

When Mac Bustos returned to Davenport, Benjamín Vázquez became the pastor. Under the leadership of Vázquez, the church split due to internal problems. When Vázquez left, Bustos took charge of both congregations.

In 1978 they obtained the services of Andrés Gallardo, a Mexican, who began with the few members who remained and soon increased the attendance to 80 persons. Gallardo was ordained to the ministry on September 30, 1979. Jaime Castañeda preached in this service with officials of the Iowa-Nebraska Conference and other pastors from the region present.

The congregation continues its outreach through a radio program called "Maranatha," which is transmitted on KSTT and directed by Pastor Gallardo.

Iglesia Evangélica Menonita
19th Street, Chicago
(Evangelical Mennonite Church of Chicago)

The work of the Chicago Home Mission, which was responsible for the first Hispanic Mennonite congregation, produced other Spanish-speaking congregations in Chicago. In 1959 the Chicago Home Mission had to move from its location on 19th Street due to the construction of the Dan Ryan Expressway. Thus, on October 18, it moved to 1113 West 18th Street and at the same time changed its name to Mennonite Community Chapel.

In spite of the changes of leadership and location, the interest of the English-speaking Mennonites in the work among Hispanics had not decreased. Conscious of the large number of Hispanics in the area they began the second phase of the Hispanic Mennonite work in Chicago. They invited Victor Ovando, who was then the pastor of the congregation in Defiance, Ohio, to begin the work. The new work stagnated several years later and today is one of the extinct congregations. Thus its history is included in the corresponding appendix.

A second more significant attempt began in 1972 when the leadership of the Mennonite Community Chapel invited Guillermo Espinoza to begin the work in the 18th Street area. Espinoza had worked with the Worldwide Evangelical Church in his native Bolivia and had recently moved to Chicago. The Espinozas, in cooperation with Miguel and Irma Torrejón, held their first service on Sunday, December 14, 1972, in one of the smallest rooms of the Mennonite Community Chapel. One week later they began to hold services on Sunday evenings at seven o'clock in the sanctuary of the church building since the English group held services only on Sunday mornings. In the beginning, William Hallman, the pastor of the Lawndale Mennonite Church, assisted in the work with the leaders and the new nucleus of believers. On Sunday, August 20 at 7:00 a.m. the first six believers were baptized in Lake Michigan. The congregation adopted the name, Evangelical Mennonite Church. By the end of the year the congregation had nine members.

On December 31, 1973, in a New Year's Eve service, the first church council was installed. The members of this were Mario Negrete, Lilia Espinoza, and Julio Arias.

The year 1974 was one of progress: thirteen new members were baptized; and the congregation began to receive economic assistance from the conference.

In January 1975, during the worker's retreat held at Camp Hebron, the congregation was accepted as an official member of the Illinois Mennonite Conference. The group continued to grow and on January 18 of that same year they held a meeting to discuss the possibilities of buying a building. After a time of searching and decision, on May 29 they purchased a funeral home for $30,000. The building located at 1021 West 19th Street was dedicated June 15. This purchase gave the congregation a spacious building with a seating capacity of 180. About this same time interest developed in establishing a new work in south Chicago. This dream became a reality with the establishment of the 51st Street church.

In 1976 Espinoza left to give pastoral leadership to the 51st Street congregation and was replaced by Joel Ortiz, who was ordained May 28, 1978. When Ortiz left he was replaced by Ramón Nieves, who served as pastor for one year. The congregation was then without a pastor for an extended period until they obtained the pastoral services of Juan Bautista Ferreras, who had served as pastor in his native Dominican Republic and on the island of Puerto Rico. The congregation is presently moving ahead briskly toward a promising future.

The 19th Street congregation has always been interested in leadership development. This has been demonstrated by the good number of young leaders that have come from this group: Samuel López, Víctor Mojica, Enrique Pacheco, and Ramiro Hernández among others.

Iglesia Menonita Hispana
(Hispanic Mennonite Church)
51st Street, Chicago

This congregation developed as an extension work of the 19th Street congregation. During 1975 a genuine desire developed to begin a Mennonite work in the southern part of the city, especially in the New City Community. There were several reasons for this interest: the 1970 census revealed the presence of a large number of Hispanics in the community; several families that attended 19th Street lived there; and there were only two small Hispanic church groups in English-speaking congregations.

As the leadership searched for a location in which to worship, history repeated itself: they found another funeral home for sale. On September 24, 1976, with financial help from the Illinois Mennonite Conference they finalized the purchase of the building at 1649 West 51st Street. Members from the 19th Street congregation helped renovate the building and it was dedicated on Saturday, October 9, 1976. Jack Stalter officiated in the name of the Illinois Mennonite Conference with others from the Moline and Chicago congregations participating. The first worship service was held the following Sunday morning.

In 1978 the first church council was selected composed of Raymundo Martínez, president; Silvia Borja, secretary; Jesús D. Anda, treasurer; María Rueda and Juanita Meléndez, deaconesses; Eustalia Peralta and Lilia Espinoza, elders, and Guillermo Espinoza, pastor.

In 1980 a series of pastor-congregation problems developed that led to the pastor's leaving in September 1982. Since that time the congregation has been without a pastor but has continued under the dynamic leadership of several members, especially that of Mrs. Norma Luna.

The Hispanic Mennonite Church of 51st Street has always been outstanding for its desire to preach the Word and minister to human need. Several examples of this missionary interest are the attempt to reopen the Hispanic work in Milwaukee, the beginning of work on 88th Street in Chicago, and the mission in Iguala, Mexico.

According to the *Mennonite Yearbook of 1983*, the Hispanic Mennonite Church of 51st Street has a present membership of 46, the majority from Mexico.

Iglesia Menonita Cristiana
(Christian Mennonite Church)
50th Street, Chicago

This congregation began in the later part of the seventies as a result of a split in the 51st Street congregation. Several pastor-congregation problems resulted in the exit of several dozen persons who then began to hold their own services elsewhere on November 20, 1979. These were held in the basement of the Eustalia Peralta home. Peralta was a member of the 51st Street congregation's church council. They immediately named Mario Portillo as their pastor. Portillo, a native of Guatemala, was then completing his theological studies. The group began to grow and the basement became quite inadequate. This forced them to look for another place to meet. They rented the building of the United Methodist Church located at 1842 West 50th Street. On December 4 of that year the building was inaugurated and the congregation chose the name Christian Mennonite Church.

In 1980 Portillo had to leave the country and the congregation was left without a pastor. Later, in December 1981, they obtained the services of Eleuterio Quiñones for six months. Today, the congregation is again without a pastor but continues under the lay leadership of Raymundo Martínez.[9]

Arizona
Iglesia Menonita Emanuel, Surprise
(Emmanuel Mennonite Church)

The Hispanic Mennonite work in the city of Surprise was begun in 1961 when the Board of Missions opened a Voluntary Service unit. Voluntary Service, which remained in Surprise until 1977, provided an activities program for youth, a kindergarten, and other social work. In 1972 Dave and Sharon Birkey felt the need to start a church. They began holding Bible studies on Sundays for women and children and after two years were able to begin worship services for interested youth and adults.

In 1975 the group, together with the Southwest Mennonite Conference, decided to begin the search for a pastor and give formal follow up to the work. They obtained the services of Atanacio Paiz, from the Mathis congregation, who was installed February 23, of that same year. Under the leadership of Paiz a ministry was initiated directed primarily to adults, and the congregation was officially organized in February 1976 when eight persons became charter members. These first members were: David and Sharon Birkey, Dave and Shelagh Rice, Julio and Mary Rodríguez, and Atanacio and Blasa Paiz. Paiz returned to Texas in July 1977 and Allan Yoder accepted the pastorate. He was ordained in June 1980 and at this writing is still pastor.

Since its beginning the group has met in a building located at 16002 North Verde Street. This building was built by the Voluntary Service unit which used it as a kindergarten. When Voluntary Service left in 1977, the building was sold to the congregation.

The enthusiastic interest in evangelism in this small congregation, which presently has 25 members, primarily Mexican Americans, has started nuclei in Peoria and Whittman. In addition it is a model with its plan for economic self-sufficiency begun in 1978.

This bilingual congregation is strategically organized into committees that effectively use the talents of the members. The present council is composed of the following: Valente Rodríguez, Ivonne Rodríguez, Bruno Montoya, Shelagh Rice, Jessie Sánchez, Aileen Herrera, José Treviño, and Tito Herrera.

New Jersey
Faro Ardiente, Vineland
(Shining Light)

On December 10, 1971, Artemio de Jesús settled in New Field, New Jersey, to begin work in the cities of Bridgeton and Norma. Already by January 1972, he began to visit homes and hold worship services in the English-speaking Mennonite church of Norma on Sunday afternoons and on Tuesday evenings. In addition he began a radio program on Sunday afternoons and a program in the migrant camps where he distributed literature and preached.

In 1973 the missionary effort was moved to the city of Vineland, where it was estimated some 16,000 Hispanics lived. They began to search for a building and one was purchased at 728 Wood Street for the sum of $20,000. After several years de Jesús resigned this pastorate in order to assume other responsibilities and challenges in the denomination. Hilario de Jesús, from the Mennonite Church of the Dominican Republic became pastor in November 1976. De Jesús served as pastor of the Shining Light congregation until he returned to the Dominican Republic. In 1982, Héctor Velázquez, who had been a leader since the time of Artemio de Jesús, assumed the pastoral responsibilities, a position he presently holds.

On September 16, 1982, this dynamic congregation, with a present membership of 66, began an outreach in Penn Grove, New Jersey, under the leadership of Angel Tamayo with the name Calvary. In addition to this accomplishment, the congregation has a music group named "Hiddekel," whose repertoire consists of "salsa" style music with Christian lyrics. This group has already recorded a long-playing record and is quite busy traveling to many U.S. churches.

Puerta de Sión, Trenton
(Door of Zion)

In October 1974, Eugenio Matos and Artemio de Jesús traveled to Trenton to start a church in that city. These first attempts produced a stable 70-member congregation that has been pastored by Matos since its beginning. The congregation, which meets at 328 South Broad Street, emphasizes prison ministries. According to the report presented by Matos at the thirteenth annual assembly of the Council of Hispanic Mennonite Churches of Pennsylvania, it presently works with some 150 Hispanic prisoners in the Bodertown Prison and another 225 in the New Jersey State Prison.

Florida

The beginning of the Hispanic Mennonite work in the state of Florida was a result of the missionary vision of the Council of Hispanic Mennonite Churches of Pennsylvania. In the spring of 1973 a delegation of the council traveled to Florida to explore the possibilities of planting churches in several locations in that state. This delegation was composed of José A. Santiago, president of the council at that time, and the leaders Ambrosio Encarnación, Isidoro Sáez, and Enrique Ayala. As a result of the investigation, the council became interested in the cities of Immokalee and Miami. Isidoro Sáez settled in the former and Enrique Ayala in the latter.

These congregations which began with ties to the Hispanic Council of Pennsylvania became affiliated with the Southeast Mennonite Convention toward the end of the seventies. This affiliation is well justified due to the distance from Pennsylvania.

It is unquestionable that the congregations in Florida have a good future due to the large number of Hispanics who live in the area.

La Puerta Hermosa, Immokalee
(Beautiful Door)

On December 5, 1973, Isidoro Sáez arrived in Immokalee, a city of some 10,000 persons, located 34 miles north of Naples and 32 miles southwest of Fort Myers. His first contacts were made with the Adorno family who were originally from Puerto Rico. They had lived in Brooklyn for twenty years where they were members of the First Mennonite Church of Brooklyn, pastored at that time by Guillermo Torres. The English-speaking Mennonite Church, People's Chapel, offered their facilities and the group began to meet on Sunday, Tuesday, and Thursday evenings.

Sáez was installed August 4, 1974, in a service led by Martin Lehman and Paul Yoder, Southeast Mennonite Convention representatives. Sáez worked hard in the community during his pastorate. On one occasion he helped facilitate Mennonite Central Committee relief work following a hurricane. He left the Immokalee congregation in October 1975 to accept the call of the Ark of Salvation congregation in Philadelphia.

Sáez was replaced by his son Johnny Sáez who was installed October 23, 1975, in a service in which Nelson Kauffman officiated. Sáez helped maintain the group that his father had started and began to give it form and unity. The first baptism was held during his term as pastor. In December 1975, six persons were baptized: Abelino Sanabria, Josefina Sanabria, Joel Sáez, Jesús Colón, José Juarbe, and Seferino Moreno. In the same service three persons were received as members by letter of transfer: Irving and Elena Pérez, and Blanca Adorno. Johnny Sáez served as pastor until December 1976.

Sáez was replaced by Irving Pérez, who began his work in January 1977. During his pastorate the congregation realized its dream of having its own place of worship when they purchased the building located at 222 North 3rd Street in August 1977. Pérez served as pastor until that same month when he moved to San Antonio, Texas, to study in the Nazarene Hispanic American Seminary.

In September of that year Juan Navarro arrived to lead the congregation. He was a member of the Church of the Good Shepherd in Lancaster, Pennsylvania. Navarro was commissioned by the Southeast Mennonite Convention on October 1, 1977. Navarro remained as pastor until December 1981. In January 1982, Abelino Sanabria, a member of the first group baptized, began to lead the congregation until they found pastoral leadership. In April 1982, Irving Pérez, who had been studying for the ministry, returned to Immokalee and took charge of the work. Pérez was installed on June 12 of that same year and continues to head that small congregation.

The Beautiful Door congregation, a name chosen from Acts 3:2, faces various problems that retard its growth: first, the constant change of leadership; second, the congregation is located in an area with a transitory population due to its dependence on agriculture.

In spite of these difficulties they are moving toward their goals.

For example, in 1982 they formulated the following: purchase a building, develop a mission work in Fort Meyers, and establish a good children's program. These goals are worthy of admiration when we note that the present membership of the congregation is only 11 persons.

Voz de Salvación, Miami
(*Voice of Salvation*)

Enrique Ayala arrived in Miami in December 1973. Upon his arrival he immediately established contacts with the English-speaking Mennonite church in the community and began to use their facilities. Thus the work developed as a Hispanic department of the English-speaking congregation in which Ayala cooperated with the pastor who led the English group.

The group began to prosper and Ayala was installed as pastor on May 4, 1974. Martin Lehman, a representative of the Southeast Mennonite Convention, officiated in the service. Ayala resigned his ministry in December 1975 and moved to Chicago. He was replaced by Ambrosio Encarnación, one of the members of the exploratory commission in the summer of 1973. Encarnación, originally from the Dominican Republic and who had moved to Pennsylvania from Puerto Rico in 1972, was installed on December 28, 1975. A short time later he was named overseer of the Hispanic Mennonite congregations in Florida. During his pastorate, the small group, which, as we have stated, was a Hispanic department of the English-speaking congregation, officially organized itself as a separate congregation. This took place in a service on November 24, 1977. Caonabo Reyes, pastor of the Hispanic Mennonite congregation of Washington, D.C., was the principal speaker while LeRoy Sheats, representing the Southeast Mennonite Convention, led the ceremony proclaiming the group to be a congregation with the name Voice of Salvation Church. Encarnación resigned this pastorate and left on October 8, 1979, to accept the pastorate of the Sarasota group.

At the present time Eugenio Romero, also from the Dominican Republic and who had been superintendent of the Sunday school for a time, took the reins of leadership of the congregation. He was installed on October 14, 1979, in a service in which Wilbur Lentz, pastor in

Anderson, South Carolina, preached and Melvin Shirk, pastor in Sarasota, officiated in the installation ceremony and licensing. Today Eugenio Romero continues as the pastor of the 20-member Miami congregation.

Iglesia Seguidores de Cristo, Sarasota
(Followers of Christ Church)

The Hispanic Mennonite church in the city of Sarasota had its beginnings as an independent congregation. Aníbal Ramos, pastor of this congregation, made contacts with the Mennonite Church through his friendship with Enrique Ayala and Isidoro Sáez, who at that time pastored the congregations of Miami and Immokalee, respectively. He became interested in the Mennonites and in 1974 his congregation became affiliated with the denomination through the Southeast Mennonite Convention and the Council of Hispanic Mennonite Churches of Pennsylvania. From this time the congregation became known as the Iglesia Menonita Avivada (Revived Mennonite Church) and met in the church building of the English-speaking Mennonite congregation, Newton Gospel Chapel. Although the group now had the name Mennonite and had officially joined the denomination, it never really entered the Mennonite world and pulled away in 1978. Many of the members joined the Only Jesus Church.

Seeing the need for a group in this city, the Hispanic leadership decided to begin another congregation. In the spring of 1979, Ramón Nieves, who was in the area, was invited to begin holding services and start a group. After three months of work he was able to begin a small group. He then left for Honduras, Central America.

In October 1979, Ambrosio Encarnación arrived in Sarasota from Miami to provide leadership for the small group. At the same time he served as the associate secretary of Latin Concerns in the Southeast Mennonite Convention. Already by November 1979, the group had acquired structure and stability and by the first Sunday in March 1980 had their first Sunday school. At that time they were using two different locations: one for Friday Bible studies and another for Sunday school. In addition they held Bible studies in different homes during the week. On July 20, 1980, they held their first baptism when Moisés and Rosa Guillén were submerged in the waters of Siesta Key Beach.

The year 1981 was one of much progress for this congregation. In January they began to meet in one location. In March they named their first council, composed of Fray Morales, president; Guillermo Torres, vice-president; Dolce Swartzendruber, treasurer; Jennie Encarnación, secretary; Fred Swartzendruber and Rosa Guillén, members at large; and Ambrosio Encarnación, pastor. On August 9, they celebrated the baptism of thirteen persons, again in Siesta Key Beach. On Sunday, October 25, they organized themselves as a congregation with the name Iglesia Seguidores de Cristo (Followers of Christ Church). This same month they began to meet in the Youth Hall of the Bahía Vista Mennonite Church.

This newborn congregation deeply dedicated to the proclamation of the Word has developed several types of ministry. Among these is a radio program called *Sarasota for Christ*, which goes on the air each Sunday at 3:30 p.m. over WKZM, FM 105.5. The first recording was made on March 6, 1982, and the first broadcast went on the air on March 21.

Ebenezer, Orlando

The congregation in Orlando began as an independent group and joined the Mennonite Church in 1982. The congregation is led by Wilson Reyes and has a membership of 14.

Washington, D.C.
Iglesia Evangélica Menonita Hispana
(Evangelical Hispanic Mennonite Church)

On July 5, 1975, Caonabo and Mireya Reyes arrived in the U.S. capital with the fervent desire to begin a work. This couple, who had been active members in the Good Shepherd Mennonite Church of Lancaster, arrived on their own and settled at 1810 16th Street in Silver Springs in the area of Summit Hills. They began to hold services in their apartment on Sundays and to visit the homes in the community. Soon they had a good number of persons attending the services.

In December 1975, they began to use the basement of the International Guest House, a Mennonite agency sponsored by the Allegheny Mennonite Conference. Due to problems with the heating system, they moved and rented a room in the All Soul's Church on the corner of Columbia Road and 16th Street. After some five months in this location they again moved since they did not feel comfortable in the Unitarian surroundings. The group of forty persons began to meet in the home of Eva Méndez.

Finally, in May 1977, the Board of Missions of the Virginia Mennonite Conference, in collaboration with the Mennonite Board of Missions, purchased a large house for $85,000 located at 5327 Northeast 16th Street. The new facilities were inaugurated on May 15. At that time the congregation offered a series of unique services to the Hispanic community of Washington, D.C.: counseling concerning how to obtain United States citizenship, job orientation, social services counseling, and English classes.

This congregation can be cataloged as a migratory one. Many of its members move frequently and some even have to leave the country which makes it difficult to develop a solid stable nucleus. For example, in 1980, there was a roundup of undocumented persons and many were deported to their home countries resulting in a considerable decrease in attendance.

In May 1982, Reyes resigned the pastorate, and Lester T. Hershey, who had worked with the Hispanic Mennonite church in its beginnings, took the leadership of the congregation.

This congregation, with its amazing amount of heterogeneity (it contains persons from El Salvador, Costa Rica, Guatemala, Dominican Republic, Puerto Rico, Bolivia, Mexico, Peru, and Uruguay) presently has six active members. However, in spite of its sudden reverses, this congregation continues to offer, in addition to Sunday worship services, a dynamic and attractive program: Bible studies in homes on Monday evenings; and prayer services at 6:00 a.m. on Wednesdays, followed by breakfast when the members have an opportunity to share.

California
Monte de Sinaí, Los Angeles
(Mount Sinai)

Even though the state of California is densely populated with Hispanics, yet the Mennonite Church had never established a definite program to work among these people. Only a few Hispanics attended English-speaking Mennonite churches. In spite of this fact, there had always been a deep interest in beginning work in this fertile terrain.

Thus, in August 1978, they obtained the services of Héctor Muñoz to begin work in Los Angeles. Muñoz, who had been a missionary in Central America and Puerto Rico, moved to the city in September 1978 and began to hold Bible studies in several homes. In January 1979, the English-speaking Mennonite congregation, Los Angeles Fellowship, pastored by Leo Egli, allowed them to use their facilities one day a week. In addition, they began to hold outdoor services in McArthur Central Park in the Mexican district. The work grew rapidly and by the summer of that year they had a Sunday attendance of 69. During this time the congregation chose the name Luz del Mundo (Light of the World).

In October 1979, Muñoz learned to know Salvador Arana, who had been a pastor in his native country of El Salvador and now wanted to work in the Lord's vineyard. Arana attended the worship services and energetically assisted Muñoz. In November 1980, Arana was licensed by the Southwest Mennonite Conference and took charge of the congregation. A short time later the name of the congregation was changed to Mount Sinai, as it is known today.

With the financial help of the conference the congregation has obtained its own church building and has a membership of 58.

House of the Lord Fellowship, La Puente

At the same time he was working in Los Angeles, Muñoz had been holding services in La Puente. The group met each Thursday in the home of Gonzalo and María Martínez. Later they met Sunday mornings in the home of Muñoz where they used the living room and bedrooms for Sunday school classes.

The group organized itself as a congregation in October 1980, choosing the name, House of the Lord Fellowship. In July 1981, they rented a house on Asuzer Avenue where they presently hold services. The services are bilingual since many of the members are young people whose vernacular is English. This congregation has a great ministry among the young drug addicts and gangs. The present attendance oscillates between 50 and 60 persons.

New Jerusalem Spanish Mennonite
North Hollywood

The missionary activity of Muñoz was not limited to Los Angeles and La Puente, but at the same time he worked in the community of North Hollywood holding services in the home of Jesús and Elizabeth Villa. Two days a week they rented the YMCA in Laurel Canyon. The group formally organized themselves as a congregation there in April 1980.

Undoubtedly, the southwestern part of the United States, and especially California, is one of the most promising with respect to the possibilities of growth and development. It is possible that California will in the next fifty years become the strong nucleus of the Hispanic Mennonite Church of North America. Only time will tell if we are mistaken or not.

New Mexico
Iglesia Evangélica Menonita, Carlsbad
(Evangelical Mennonite Church)

The Hispanic Mennonite work in Carlsbad began as a result of the missionary vision of the local Mennonite congregation, the Rocky Mountain Mennonite Conference and the Mennonite Board of Missions. Raymundo Gómez was designated to begin the work and arrived in Carlsbad on June 3, 1979. Gómez, who had been assistant pastor in Moline, Illinois congregation, began to hold services in the facilities of the Mennonite Church of Carlsbad, located at 1301 West McKay Street and pastored by Peter Hartman. Their hours for worship alternate with those of the English-speaking congregation. The group began to take shape: Gómez was installed near the end of 1979 and the congregation was officially organized on October 26, 1980.

The program of this small congregation is varied and dynamic. It includes a radio program that goes out over the air every Saturday at 8:30 a.m., home visitation, weekly Bible studies, two Sunday services, chaplaincy in a local hospital, and ministry to prison inmates. The attendance of this young congregation with a membership of 9 sometimes reaches 42.

Delaware
Centro de Amor Cristiano, Wilmington
(Center of Christian Love)

In December 1981, Juan Vega settled in Wilmington for the purpose of beginning a Hispanic work. After several months of work and the formation of a small nucleus, he left in August 1982 for Guatemala to work with the Mennonite Church of that country. He was replaced in September of that year by Rosemberg Rojas, who had pastored for several years in the Lancaster congregation.

At the present moment the attendance of this beginning congregation sometimes reaches 20 persons. The prospects of progress are heartening.

Michigan
Templo Menonita de la Hermosa, Kalamazoo
(Beautiful Mennonite Temple)

In March 1982, Teófilo Ponce, who began the work in Marion and labored decisively in the Goshen congregation, initiated a residential census of the city of Kalamazoo. In April he began to hold services in several homes twice a month and by July he was holding services every Sunday. On December 5, 1982, he began to hold services on Sunday afternoons in the Stockbridge United Methodist Church, 1331 South Rice Street. A group from the Goshen congregation participated in the first service which had an attendance of 25 people.

Ponce, who was ordained in a special service on May 15, 1983, began the work without economic assistance from any organization. Today, he receives support from the Mennonite Board of Missions and from the Missions Commission of the Indiana-Michigan Mennonite Conference.

Canada
Iglesia Evangélica, Edmonton, Alberta
(Evangelical Church)

On July 26, 1975, a meeting of Hispanic evangelicals was held in Edmonton. This gathering was for the purpose of discussing the situation of the evangelical church in Chile and serve as a forum for the interchange of ideas concerning the function of an evangelical group. Jorge and Hipólito Vallejos were put in charge of organizing further meetings. Nine persons attended this first activity.

When the leaders saw that the people were not open to meeting in individual homes, they began to look for a church building in which to meet. In October they obtained the facilities of the Evangelical Church of Richmond Park. The group began to take shape and acquire stability and on February 27, 1976, three persons publicly received Christ as their personal Savior. Already by June 1976, a group of eight persons was baptized: Rafael and Pilar Barahona, Raúl and Margarita Valenzuela, Delia Pérez, Carlos Fenixia, and Daniel Rojas. In that same month pastor Jorge Vallejos resigned his employment in the Alberta Oil Tool Company and dedicated full time to the pastorate.

Then in May 1979, they learned to know Nancy Hostetler, who introduced them to the Mennonite denomination. Hostetler, who knew Spanish very well through her many years of missionary work in Puerto Rico, served as an intermediary between the congregation and the Northwest Conference of the Mennonite Church. The congregation already faced problems with the use of the above-mentioned church building, so in October 1979 they began to use the facilities of the Holyrood Mennonite Church located at 9505 79th Street in Edmonton.

The congregation, which began as an independent group, officially joined the Mennonite Church in July 1982. This relationship has not been limited to Canada, since, recently, several congregations in Chile in which Vallejos had ministered also joined the denomination.

Iglesia Evangélica, Calgary, Alberta
(Evangelical Church)

The Calgary congregation, begun in the summer of 1978, also joined the conference in July 1982. It presently uses the facilities of the Mennonite English-speaking Calgary Fellowship congregation and is pastored by Hipólito Vallejos. This young congregation has a membership of 60.

These Canadian congregations primarily serve people from Chile since they compose 80 percent of the Hispanic population of those areas. However, they have many members from other Central and South American countries such as Peru, Ecuador, Colombia, and El Salvador.

In addition to the two congregations already mentioned, a third has just been started and, therefore, is still in the embryonic stage. Juan Iturriaga, a native of Chile and director of the House of Friendship program in Montreal, attended the VI Convention of Hispanic Mennonite Churches held in Hesston in August 1982. The experience of being able to praise the Lord in his own tongue led him to leave determined to begin a Hispanic work in Montreal, Quebec. Inaugural services were held October 29-31 in which brothers and sisters from Canadian and U.S. congregations participated.

This historical review of the congregations that make up the family of the Hispanic Mennonite Churches of North America hopefully provides a clear portrait of the many and varied elements that have been part of this challenging fifty-year history. In every congregation there have been unique leaders, different contexts, and varied motives. But indisputably there has always been a clear and precise purpose that has motivated and energized them all: to take the Word of life to the Hispanics that live in the United States and Canada.

AGENCIES, ASSOCIATIONS, AND PROGRAMS

5
AGENCIES, ASSOCIATIONS, AND PROGRAMS

As is natural in the development of any vital organization, basic agencies, associations, and programs develop that complement it. In the specific case of the Hispanic Mennonite Church of North America a variety of organizations came to life during the years of thrust and organization, especially during the decade of the seventies. These organizations have contributed immeasurably to provide a foundation and guidelines for a prosperous church worthy of praise and emulation.

Hispanic Mennonite Women's Conference

The first meeting of the Hispanic Mennonite women was held April 14, 1973, in the Moline church. Women from Illinois, Indiana, Texas, and New York were present in this activity, organized by María Snyder, Mary Bustos and Lupe Bustos. This historic activity, in which Snyder was the principal speaker, ended with a precious and significant communion service.

These women met with a series of objectives in mind: develop a program in Spanish, encourage one another, share as Hispanic women, and open paths of communication between the various Hispanic women's groups in the nation.

In October 1973, the first Hispanic Workers Retreat was held in Sandia, Texas, and the women who attended took advantage of the opportunity to meet together. On this occasion they decided that they wanted to continue holding inspirational meetings such as they had

had in Moline. They then proceeded to name Mary Bustos as coordinator of the activity which they decided to hold in Lancaster, Pennsylvania, in 1974. In addition they named María Snyder, Cecilia Robinson and Mary Valtierra as members of the steering committee that would work with Bustos.

The theme of the Lancaster meeting was "A Determined Woman in a Hostile Environment" with the principal speaker, Lilia Espinoza, basing her talks on the book of Esther. This meeting produced several important decisions. They decided to hold biennial meetings. They changed the name, which initially was Services of Inspiration, to Hispanic Mennonite Women's Conference, and Mary Bustos was again named coordinator for the 1976 conference.

The third conference was held April 9-11, 1976, in Corpus Christi, Texas. The principal speaker was Cecilio Arrastía, who developed the theme of "Ambassadors of Christ," based on 2 Corinthians 5:20. Delegates from eighteen women's groups were present with one hundred persons attending the activities.

The fourth conference was held at Goshen College April 27 to 30, 1978, coordinated by María Snyder. Julia Campos was the speaker for the occasion and developed the theme "The Liberty and Responsibility of the Christian Family" based on Deuteronomy 11:18-21. A lovely and meaningful booklet containing many photographs and several articles by Hispanic leaders of the denomination was published as a souvenir of the occasion.

Camp Menno Haven in Tiskilwa, Illinois, was the location of the fifth conference coordinated by Elizabeth Pérez. The theme of this activity, held April 24-27, 1980, was "The Power of the Christian Woman." Linda Buller, who had lived for some time in Colombia, was the principal speaker for the 140 women that attended. María Elena Ruiz, of San Antonio, Texas, was in charge of the special music. In that meeting they adopted the abbreviation SDCA, Sociedad de Damas Cristianas en Acción (Society of Christian Women in Action) to replace the previous name of WMSC (Women's Missionary and Service Commission). Twenty-six delegates attended with a total attendance that varied between 150 and 160 persons.

The sixth Hispanic Women's Conference was held in Denton, Texas, April 15-18, 1982. The 125 women that attended enjoyed the presentations of Marta C. Escobar based on the theme "The Woman Subject to the Holy Spirit." Special music for the activity was provided by the group, Los Emanuel, of Corpus Christi, Texas. Seferina De León and Mary Bustos were named representatives to the Mennonite World Conference to be held in France in August 1984. The organization of the conference was in charge of the Executive Committee composed of Seferina De León, coordinator; Clarita Gómez, Luisa Tijerina, and Mary Bustos; and by the subcommittees headed by Esther Hinojosa, Elizabeth Pérez, María Tijerina, and Belinda Bustos.

Elections for the different official responsibilities during the 82-84 biennium produced the following: Seferina De León, WMSC representative; Luisa Tijerina, 1984 conference coordinator. The following area secretaries were elected: Minnie Del Río (Ohio), Belinda Bustos (Iowa), María Ortiz (New York), Elizabeth Pérez (Texas), Elena Pérez (Florida), and Yolanda Limar (Oregon).

In its first decade of life the Women's Conference has grown with steady steps. Sixty persons attended the first assembly while in the last conference the attendance reached one hundred and twenty-five. Eleven groups were represented in the first meeting and twenty-four in the last. Economically speaking, in that first year, 1973, all was accomplished through faith while today funds are received from various denominational agencies but with the clear goal of future economic independence.

Office of Latin Concerns

The Office of Latin Concerns began its work during the first week of August 1974, under the leadership of the newly named associate general secretary, José M. Ortiz. At that time the office was located in Rosemont, near the Chicago O'Hare Airport. In October it was moved to Lombard to the annex of the Lombard Mennonite Church. Freida Myers served as secretary and General Secretary Paul Kraybill as supervisor. In 1977 Kraybill was replaced by Ivan Kauffmann who continues to serve in that position.

In its attempt to promote solidarity and communication the office began to publish an informative bulletin called *Ahora (Now)*. The editor, Ortiz himself, wrote in the first issue:

This is the first issue of *Ahora*. It is to be an attempt to inform you about what is happening "here and now" in our office. It will be sent to pastors and lay leaders with comments and announcements of interest to our Hispanic leadership. Since it is directed to the leadership it will not compete with nor attempt to replace *Ecos Menonitas (Mennonite Echos)* but will supplement the communication process. Look for it each month.

This bulletin continues to be published fulfilling its purpose.

The Office of Latin Affairs was moved to the central Mennonite offices in Elkhart, Indiana, in 1977 due to the conveniences of being closer to the agencies and organizations that serve the church in general. The offices first were located on the third floor of the Greencroft building and later transferred to the second floor. Rachel Good was hired as assistant administrator. When Good resigned she was replaced by Frances Eash and she, in turn, by Bea Blosser who continues in that position.

After serving eight years, José M. Ortiz resigned as associate general secretary in August 1982. He was replaced by Samuel Hernández, who continues to serve in that capacity.

The agenda of the office includes a number of vital functions: (1) plan, develop, and implement the decisions of the biennial conventions; (2) represent the interests of the Hispanic Church before the Mennonite Church, its agencies, and committees; (3) identify general needs of the church and look for ways to meet these needs; and (4) organize the Administrative Committee meetings and provide follow-up for the recommendations that come from these meetings.

The Comité Administrativo (Administrative Committee), previously known as the Concilio Latino (Latin Council), is the organization that is responsible for the oversight and direction of the Office of Latin Concerns. The committee is composed of seven members that according to the constitution are selected in the following manner: a representative from each of the North American geographical regions that have Hispanic Mennonite work, a representative from the Hispanic Women's Conference, and two representatives elected by the Convention. The following individuals have served as president of the administrative committee: Mac Bustos, Armando Calderón, Samuel Hernández, Conrado Hinojosa, and the present incumbent, Elías

Pérez. In addition to Pérez the present committee is composed of Héctor Vázquez, vice-president; José Mojica, José A. Santiago, Maggie De León, secretary; Artemio de Jesús and Luisa Tijerina.

It is not necessary to point out the importance of this office. It is sufficient to mention that it has held a central place in the development of the history related in these pages.

Office of Congregational Education and Literature in Spanish

In a meeting in February 1974, the obvious need for literature in Spanish led the National Council to name a steering committee to work toward this end. The committee held its first meeting November 8-9, 1974, in the Imperial 400 Motel in Chicago. The committee was composed of Mary Bustos, Arnoldo Casas, Guillermo Espinoza, Lupe García, Frank Ventura, and Caonabo Reyes, in addition to several representatives of the pertinent denominational agencies, such as David Helmuth (Board of Congregational Ministries), Lawrence Martin (Mennonite Publishing House), and Lupe De León (Home Missions). This committee investigated the availability of literature in Spanish, Spanish publishing houses, and Spanish literature distribution centers. In addition it began to study the possibility of publishing an informative periodical for national distribution. This idea became what is known today as the periodical *Ecos Menonitas (Mennonite Echos)*, which was first published in January 1975. This periodical continues to be published every three months and is distributed in North America, South America, the Caribbean, and Spain.

The above-mentioned committee worked until August 1976, when it was dissolved to open the way for the newly created Office of Congregational Education and Literature in Spanish. This commission would function under the auspices of the Mennonite Board of Congregational Ministries and the direction of the associate secretary, Arnoldo Casas. The office has several objectives: provide good literature in Spanish, curricular and informative material, as well as other resources; provide leadership in the preparation of Christian education teachers; and coordinate activities related to family life.

The work of the associate secretary is complimented by the Office of Congregational Education and Literature in Spanish, composed of Rafael Falcón, president; Angel Pérez, secretary; Lupe García, Ray González, and Jenny Encarnación. Others who have worked on the commission are Enriqueta Díaz, Sila Oliva, Rolando Santiago, Rubén Esquivel, and Gloria Cornejo. This commission has several very important responsibilities: advise the Mennonite Board of Congregational Ministries, the Mennonite Publishing House and its personnel in relation to the development of an adequate philosophy of congregational biblical education; advise said agencies concerning congregational study materials; and advise the Mennonite Publishing House concerning the promotion and marketing of literature in Spanish.

In addition to the already mentioned commission, the office works with the editorial commission of *Ecos Menonitas*. This commission is composed of Víctor Mojica, Noemí Santiago, Daniel Pérez, Eliel Núñez, and Sandra Güete. Others that have worked on this commission are Jacobo Tijerina, Margarita Mojica, Gerardo Mojica, and Irving Pérez. This commission has the function of working together with the editor in the editorial and conceptual composition of the periodical.

Through the Mennonite Publishing House the office has facilitated the publication of a substantial number of books, some originally in Spanish and others translated from English. Some of these titles are the new edition of *Menno Simons: His Life and Writings* (1979); several J. C. Wenger booklets from the Mennonite Faith Series (1979)—*The Way to a New Life, How Mennonites Came to Be, The Way of Peace, What Mennonites Believe,* and *Disciples of Jesus*—, *La familia hispana y su relación en el contexto cristiano (The Hispanic Family and Its Relationships in the Christian Context)* (1979)—a series of essays that were presented in the family life retreat in Leaky, Texas; and *Tomás y los Pájaros Parlantes* (1979)—a translation of the children's book by Ruth Nulton Moore, *Tomás and the Talking Birds*. In addition a series of Bible study guides has been published including *The Holy Spirit in the Life of the Church, Biblical Interpretation in the Life of the Church, Parables of the Kingdom,* and *Affirming Our Faith in Word and Deed*.

The office has coordinated several significant congregational education activities in Iowa, Texas, Indiana, and Pennsylvania.

Outstanding among these were the teacher training workshop in Davenport, Iowa, in June 1979 and the family life workshop in Leaky, Texas, in September of the same year.

This nationally based office has played a principal part in the beginning and development of the inter-Mennonite Hispanic American project that is known today as Currículo Anabautista de Educación Bíblica Congregacional (Anabaptist Curriculum of Congregational Biblical Education) with the purpose of producing a curriculum with an Anabaptist base for the Latin American context.

Arnoldo Casas is the present executive director of the project that is governed by an executive board composed of Lupe De León (U.S.), president; Gilberto Flores (Guatemala), vice-president; Marta Quiroga de Alvarez (Argentina), secretary; Carlos Escobar Gutiérrez (Mexico), auditor; Fabiola A. de Rodríquez (Colombia), member at large; and Federico Rosado (Puerto Rico), member at large. In addition to these persons the project includes Héctor Valencia, editorial director; and Rafael Falcón, Milka Rindzinski, and Gilberto Flores, north, south, and central editors, respectively.

Clearly the Office of Congregational Education and Literature in Spanish has and will continue to have a principal role in the development of the Hispanic Mennonite Church of North America. It has filled a vacuum that has existed for 44 years. This is the factor that impeded a more accelerated development in this first stage.

Mennonite Hispanic Immigration Service

It is conservatively estimated that between 5 and 8 million undocumented people presently live in the United States. In 1976 more than 800,000 were deported by Naturalization and Immigration Service agents. Of these 90 percent were from Mexico.

Since the Hispanic Mennonite Church does not escape the dilemma of the undocumented, a group of pastors and leaders who were interested in this captivating and challenging problem met at Laurelville, Pennsylvania, in October 1976 to discuss this issue. The interest in and urgency of the problem led Home Missions to organize a three-day seminar in Washington, D.C. As a result of the recommendations that came from this seminar, an office was established that is known today as Servicio de Emigración Menonita Hispano

(Mennonite Hispanic Immigration Service). The office, located in the Methodist Building at 100 Northeast Maryland Avenue, Washington, D.C., opened its doors to the public in February 1978. It is administered by Mennonite Central Committee, which employed Karen Ventura as consultant and director.

Hispanic Mennonite Immigration Service was established with several primary objectives in mind: serve as a resource center to the Mennonite Church for information pertaining to laws and governmental proposals related to immigration; provide direct assistance— legal services, contacts, etc.—to members of the church who face immigration problems; and sponsor educational workshops for persons with interest in this area.

From January 31 to February 2, 1980, the office sponsored a training workshop in which ten persons participated. The workshop was the first step in the establishment of a chain of persons who would work with the congregations as regional contacts. In this way these persons would work as regional representatives with members eligible to receive immigration benefits and would provide informational resources for their congregations and communities. In addition the workshop sought to establish the steps the church would need to take in order to have its voice heard in issues related to immigration. Nine resolutions were produced by this workshop that have promoted the development of the office.[1] The participants in this activity were: Ambrosio Encarnación (Florida), Andrés Gallardo (Iowa), Pastor Mateo (New York), Teófilo Ponce (Indiana), Samuel Reséndez (California), Caonabo Reyes (Washington, D.C.), Elisa Santiago (California), Rolando Santiago (Pennsylvania), César Segura (Pennsylvania), and Christian Yoder (Texas).

In 1981, as a result of the efforts that began in January 1980, Hispanic Mennonite Immigration Service was accredited by the Immigration Board of the Department of Justice of the United States as a nonprofit organization which can represent immigrants in legal proceedings.

Karen Ventura, who had administered the office since its beginnings, resigned in 1982. She was replaced by Carlos Neuschwander, who began his work August 23 of that same year and continues to serve in that capacity.

Hispanic Ministries Department

The Hispanic Mennonite leadership had been expressing its concern for the theological training of church leaders since the beginning of the decade of the seventies, and specifically in 1974 when they formed the institute-on-wheels committee. However, it was not until 1976 that the elements began to appear that would result in the solid program that exists today. In November of that year, Home Missions provided the first $10,000 designated for Hispanic Mennonite theological training. Other agencies followed in their steps.

Interest and need, together with the economic resources now made available, resulted in a program sponsored by Hesston College and the National Council, located at the Nazarene Hispanic American Seminary. The program was directed by Victor Alvarez and began to function in September 1977, with a dozen students. As a result of several incidents, the council began to realize that the students should receive their training in a totally Mennonite context. After consulting with the leadership of Hesston College the program was expanded and moved to Goshen College in 1979.

The Hispanic Ministries Department, as it will be known from this moment, is sponsored conjointly by the Mennonite Board of Education, the Mennonite Church General Board, the Associated Mennonite Biblical Seminaries, and the National Council of Hispanic Mennonite Churches. Rafael Falcón was named to direct the program and teach, and Lourdes Miranda to teach six courses per year. Falcón arrived in Goshen July 13, 1979, and on September 12 the program officially began with the start of the new academic year. In that historic fall trimester sixteen students appeared on the list of the newly created Department: Héctor Vázquez, Eva Vázquez, Samuel López, Ramiro Hernández, Marta Hernández, Leoncio Gutiérrez, all who had transferred from the program in the Nazarene Seminary, and new students David Acosta, Miguel A. Cruz, Fidencia Flores, Eliel Núñez, Margarita Pequeño, Daniel Pérez, Orlando Rivera, Elizabeth Santiago, and Alfa Tijerina.

The department formulated the following objectives: (1) prepare pastors for Hispanic Mennonite congregations who will be competent in biblical interpretation, preaching, counseling, Christian education, evangelism, and church planting, organization, and administration;

(2) prepare Hispanic Mennonite students for congregational and community leadership; (3) train students in oral and written skills both in English and Spanish; (4) provide the possibility of combining the development of pastoral and lay leadership with general education and professional preparation; and (5) help students understand and appreciate Hispanic and Hispanic Mennonite culture and experience.

The students may major, co-major, or complete a certificate program in Hispanic ministries. The major is designed primarily for students interested in pastoral ministry or for pastors who want to develop their leadership and Bible study abilities. The co-major in Hispanic ministries can be combined with another major such as primary education, communications, economics, or social work for the purpose of preparing the student both for congregational and for community leadership. The two-year certificate program (60 credit hours), which was begun in 1982-83, is designed for more mature pastors or lay leaders who wish to study only in Spanish, or who do not wish to matriculate in a baccalaureate program. The departmental classes are offered in Spanish while the other college classes are in English, so students develop oral and written skills in both languages. The departmental curriculum offers several classes that are designed specifically for the Hispanic Mennonite milieu, such as Hispanic Mennonite History, Hispanic Culture and Society, Hispanic Family Life, and Hispanic Peace Team.

The students have come from many different parts of the United States: Chicago, Goshen, Defiance, Lancaster, New York, Immokalee, Alice, and Vineland. Others have come from overseas: the Dominican Republic, Bolivia, Venezuela, Colombia, Costa Rica, Puerto Rico, and Honduras. The number of students has fluctuated during the first years as is shown by the chart on next page.

As can be seen, the lowest number of students was 16 in the fall of 1979-80, the first group, and that the largest number, 32, was in the fall of 1981-82. Of the dozens of students that have passed through its halls, twenty have graduated, completing either a baccalaureate degree or a certificate. The first graduate was Samuel López, from Chicago, in the fall of 1980-81. The graduates today occupy a variety of positions: some are pastors, postgraduate students, nurses, administrators, etc.

Year	Fall	Winter	Spring	Graduates
1979-80	16	19	19	0
1980-81	25	26	26	3
1981-82	32	29	29	8
1982-83	25	23	23	9

In addition to the persons already mentioned, others have collaborated in the department: Ronald Collins, who replaced Miranda in 1981, and José M. Ortiz, Lupe De León, Angel Luis Miranda, Atlee Beechy, and David Helmuth who have taught part time in the program.

The program receives counsel from the Hispanic Ministries Coordinating Committee. This committee is composed of the following 11 members: one of the presidents of the Associated Mennonite Biblical Seminaries, a Seminary student, two National Council representatives, a General Conference Mennonite Church representative, a Goshen College administration representative, a Mennonite Central Committee representative, a Mennonite Board of Missions representative, a Hispanic Ministries student, the associate general secretary for Latin Concerns and the director of the department. The committee meets once a year.

It is unquestionable that the Hispanic Ministries Department has filled a vacuum in the life of the Hispanic Mennonite Church. This is based on the fact that it is extremely difficult, if not impossible, to develop a genuine Mennonite church without leaders trained in the foundation that is taught and the name that is proclaimed.

High-Aim

The High-Aim program officially began in 1968 for the purpose of providing minority students with the opportunity to attend a Mennonite high school. It was thought that giving the minority student a solid education would aid leadership development for the life and mission of the church. The philosophy of the program was stated thus:

> Minority persons in the Mennonite Church face the challenge of relating their cultures and personalities to the life and mission of the Anabaptist-Mennonite faith. It is appropriate that the Mennonite Church, through its high schools, encourage minority young people to begin to define what being Anabaptist-Mennonite Christians means for them.[2]

High-Aim was the product of the efforts of several individuals. However, Lee Roy Berry was the person primarily responsible for the birth of the program. Berry considered that he had received an important step forward in life due to his educational experience at Eastern Mennonite College. He pointed out that if other blacks would have similar opportunities they could escape the poverty cycle. In addition he thought that an integrated program could help both the minorities and the majority relate to and understand each other better.

In 1969 the Mennonite Board of Missions became involved in the program and gave it the name, High-Aim. "High" for "high school" and "Aim" for "Associates in Mission," who provided the financial help in the beginning. Clearly the name would stimulate the students to aim high.

The program, adopted by the Relief and Service Division of the Mennonite Board of Missions named Gene Yoder as its first coordinator in October 1970. Lupe García, the first Hispanic director, began his work in June 1972 and served until June 1975. García was followed by Art Griffin, who directed the program until December 1976. In July 1976, during the administration of Griffin, the program was transferred to the Mennonite Board of Education. In January 1977, Leamon Sowell, Jr., and his administration, under the umbrella of the Mennonite Board of Education, brought a number of valuable and significant changes. Sowell left in July 1978, and was replaced in August by the second Hispanic director, Irving Pérez. The administration of Pérez was short since he resigned in April 1979, to continue his college work. In September 1979, the program came under the leadership of Al Brown, who continues in that position.

When the program began in 1968, only three students participated: two girls attended Central Christian High School in Ohio, and one attended Eastern Mennonite High School in Virginia. Today the program has an average of 50 to 60 students each year, of which about half are Hispanics, and the participation of seven high schools: Bethany Christian High School, Goshen, Indiana; Christopher Dock High School, Lansdale, Pennsylvania; Eastern Mennonite High School, Harrisonburg, Virginia; Iowa Mennonite School, Kalona, Iowa; Lancaster Mennonite School, Lancaster, Pennsylvania; Western Mennonite School, Salem, Oregon; and Central Christian High School, Kidron, Ohio.

The program has an Advising Committee whose five members are appointed by the Mennonite Board of Education. Three are named in consultation with the Hispanic Council, the Afro-American Mennonite Association and the Mennonite Secondary Education Council. In the winter of 1982 the committee was composed of Gerald Hughes, Norman Yoder, Pleas Broaddus, Daniel Bueno, and Alfa Tijerina. The last two were named as the Hispanic representatives.

It is unquestionable that the student who participates in this program has access to many benefits among which are the following: a Christian education in a Mennonite high school; familiarization with persons from other socio-economic backgrounds; growth realized through a new motivation to learn in the context of a Christian community; the discovery of a useful place in society; and the overcoming of the economic and psychological poverty so present in the large metropolitan centers.

Hispanic Mennonite Broadcasters Association
Toward the end of 1982 the Hispanic Mennonite Broadcasters Association was formed. This group, led by Goshen College student Elías Acosta, is composed of persons that work in radio and television ministries. The Board of Directors is composed of Raymundo Gómez, New Mexico; Samuel Hernández, Indiana; and Acosta himself, presently at Goshen College. The Association has several objectives: bring together persons interested in mass communication, learn to know their needs, and provide resources for the creation of better pro-

grams. In pursuit of this last objectives the Association has sponsored television workshops in Muscatine, Iowa, and in Los Angeles, California.

This association demonstrated its usefulness at a time when radio and television ministries are an integral part of many of the congregations of the North American Hispanic Mennonite family.

It can be appreciated that the seven organizations described here have played an essential part in the development of the Hispanic church and will continue to participate in the accomplishment of the goals that the church has before it.

GROWTH AND CHALLENGE

6
GROWTH AND CHALLENGE

Growth

Looking back on the Hispanic Mennonite work leads to the conclusion that there has been phenomenal growth. Without doubt this fact is worth mentioning and analyzing.

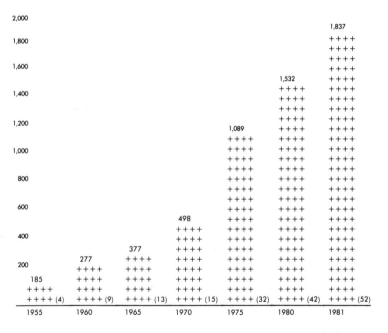

	1955	1960	1965	1970	1975	1980	1981
2,000							
							1,837
1,800							++++
							++++
							++++
1,600							++++
						1,532	++++
1,400						++++	++++
						++++	++++
						++++	++++
1,200						++++	++++
					1,089	++++	++++
					++++	++++	++++
1,000					++++	++++	++++
					++++	++++	++++
					++++	++++	++++
800					++++	++++	++++
					++++	++++	++++
					++++	++++	++++
600					++++	++++	++++
				498	++++	++++	++++
				++++	++++	++++	++++
400				++++	++++	++++	++++
			377	++++	++++	++++	++++
		277	++++	++++	++++	++++	++++
200		++++	++++	++++	++++	++++	++++
	185	++++	++++	++++	++++	++++	++++
	++++	++++	++++	++++	++++	++++	++++
	++++ (4)	++++ (9)	++++ (13)	++++ (15)	++++ (32)	++++ (42)	++++ (52)

++++ Membership
( ) Congregations

This table pictures the growth of the Hispanic Mennonite Church, but above all, the gigantic growth of the last decade. During the period from 1970 to 75 both the membership and the number of congregations doubled. Then in the period from 1975 to 1981 this phenomena almost happened again.

It should be worthwhile to analyze the situation and establish the reason for this gigantic growth. An attempt will be made to answer this interesting and difficult question based on six different particulars which do not necessarily appear in order of priority.

Organization

The organization of a Hispanic council in 1969; the employment of Lupe De León as associate secretary of the Minority Ministries Council (in Latin Concerns); the first Hispanic meeting in Sandía Texas (Zephyr Baptist Encampment) in 1973; the appointment of José M. Ortiz as associate general secretary of Latin Concerns and Lupe De León as associate secretary of Home Missions, both in 1974; the establishment of the Office of Congregational Education and Literature in Spanish in 1976 under the leadership of Arnoldo Casas; and the establishment of the Hispanic Ministries Department at Goshen College, are without doubt primary contributing factors to the growth of the Hispanic church. This is supported by the fact that the period of major growth has been precisely in this period of history which has been called the "years of organization."

The Great Commission

"Go ye therefore, and teach all nations, baptizing them in the name of the Father, and of the Son, and of the Holy Ghost" (Matthew 28:19). The soul-winning spirit of the Spanish colonizers seems to have left its imprint on the Hispanics. The center of the church's work is to preach the Word of God, the other things are either additions or related to the command of this well-known passage in Matthew. This attitude is precious and envied by many Christians today but it brings with it a particular malady: one becomes stuck at this stage and the new faith is not nurtured, the steps to growth in this "new love of Jesus Christ" are not taught.

In March 1982, during a presentation at the Associated Mennonite Biblical Seminaries in Elkhart, Indiana, on the theme of Christian nurture from a Hispanic perspective I pointed out that many times the Hispanic Mennonite continues to feed the members with "spiritual milk" and never gives them any substantial "meat." Thus there has been a stagnation at the salvation stage of Christian experience. However, on the other side, there are several healthy characteristics associated with this process. The members go out and fervently spread the Word of life in every corner of their world: the streets, supermarkets, hotels, parking lots, hospitals, factories, prisons, elevators. Without fear they speak of human sin, the forgiving grace of God, and the need of repentance to receive eternal life.

With time, with the results of the "organizational years," and with the blessing and the leading of God, I believe that a balance will come between evangelism and nurture in the Hispanic church. This last decade has given the church several key elements: a wealth of books in Spanish; the magazine *Ecos Menonitas;* the production of an Anabaptist Curriculum of Congregational Biblical Education; a Hispanic Peace Team from Goshen College, which in the last two years has confronted over 300 Hispanic youth and adults with the biblical message of peace; and a theological training program designed for lay persons and pastors.

A Favorable Clientele and Sociology

Sociologists who are experts in migratory movements point out that persons in transition are perfect targets for conversion to Christianity. Hispanics migrate to the United States with the idea that they are coming to the "land of promise," but immediately they experience the bitter reality that surrounds and assaults them. Thus the frustrations that they suffer are compensated for by the church, a community that can give them genuine and effective consolation for their difficult experiences. The Hispanic church is ready to serve this dispossessed, alienated, and uprooted clientele, and has obtained positive results.

Those who have ministered in the North American Hispanic world have been able to confirm that they work primarily with persons from a humble background in search of a place of shelter where they can put down their roots. However, it might be asked, how long will this last, since second-, third-, and forth-generation Hispanics feel more at home, have greater material security, and therefore less inclination for the gospel.

But to this must be added the fact that every day more Hispanics arrive in the United States and thus the harvest fields are increasing and the possibilities of evangelization greater.

The Enterprising Vision of the Hispanic Mennonite Pastors

The general idea of planting churches or serving as a missionary somewhere is usually accompanied by the need to present detailed budgets to the relevant institutions and wait months, and sometimes years, until the project is approved and included in the annual budget. It is true that the moral and financial support of the church institutions is needed in order to be able to go out and minister. Many Hispanic Mennonite pastors have ignored this fact and have impetuously ventured out and established missions in places where they sense the need at that particular moment.

Teófilo Ponce is a living example of this procedure. He has been responsible for the establishment of congregations such as the ones in Goshen and Marion, Indiana, and Kalamazoo, Michigan. Talking with Ponce it was learned that he did not wait for money to be approved even for his travel expenses between Middlebury, Indiana, where he lives, and the location of the work. "There is no time to waste. We must push ahead, with or without help," was the concern that Ponce communicated that Sunday evening after the evening service.

Others also model this enterprising spirit that must, whatever the place, take the message of God to the world: Caonabo Reyes, José A. Santiago, Mac Bustos, and Samuel Hernández, to mention only a few. They have to share the gift of God. Many Hispanic Mennonite pastors may not have master's nor bachelor's degrees, nor perhaps even a high school diploma, yet unquestionably they possess an untiring and energetic desire to spread the Word of a living God who loves and has transformed them.

Renewal

Much of the growth in the last ten years has occurred in the congregations where there has been an experience of renewal with a clear manifestation of the gifts of the Holy Spirit. The congregations in Pennsylvania, Florida, and California are good examples. It is my opinion that the fear that used to exist of being different in worship patterns that are outside of the traditional norms of the Mennonite Church has been slowly disappearing. Now many of the pastors express themselves freely and demonstrate that their ministry is a result of the Holy Spirit. In the conventions that are held every two years one can sense the freedom that is experienced as well as respect for the more conservative.

A Spirit of Self-identity and Independence

No longer do the Hispanics see being Mennonite as something imposed by foreigners, but as indigenous and natural. The Hispanic leader knows the Hispanic, his strengths and weaknesses; and has often had the same frustrating experiences as his clientele: problems with language, culture, and climate. These factors bring him closer to, and help him identify with, his congregation and make his ministry more effective, since his message is not just theory. It is tangible and practical.

At the present time a few Anglo pastors are still involved in the Hispanic work but if the practice which the Mennonite Church employs overseas is followed and if the Hispanic Council's desire for self-identity becomes a reality, soon the Hispanic Mennonite Church should have a totally autonomous leadership. This was once considered to be a radical concept, but now it is seen as a more feasible strategy, which has been explained positively and clearly in the previous paragraph. The formula is clear and simple: Hispanic pastors and lay persons for Hispanic programs.

The church is presently working toward the goal of independence and is exploring changes in structure that will be applicable in the coming years. I believe that the Hispanic Mennonite Church is ready for this because it has already been demonstrated in several ways. However, its economic dependence on the Anglo church plays an important part in the form, the place, and the time that this desire will become a reality.

Now it would be worthwhile to make several comments about the people that are filling the Hispanic churches. Who are they? The

Hispanic Mennonite family is composed of a great and interesting diversity of national backgrounds; Mexicans, Mexican-Americans (or Chicanos), Puerto Ricans, Dominicans, Cubans, Colombians, Costa Ricans, Bolivians, Chileans, Hondurans, Salvadorans, Guatemalans, Argentineans, and Venezuelans. The dominant groups from all of these ethnic backgrounds are the Mexicans and the Puerto Ricans. This Mexican-Puerto Rican predominance is due to the fact that of the 20 million Hispanics in the United States, the majority belong to these two ethnic backgrounds. This is understandable when we note that Puerto Ricans have had United States citizenship since 1917 and therefore can travel freely to the continent; and the Mexicans, in addition to being neighbors, occupied for centuries what is now known as the southwestern part of the United States.

It is interesting to note that each group has its area of predominance: the Mexicans in California and Texas, the Puerto Ricans in New York and Pennsylvania, the Cubans and Dominicans in Florida, and the Chileans in Canada.

Heterogeneity in the Hispanic Mennonite Church is also apparent in the cultural, linguistic, educational, religious, and social backgrounds. These elements do not simplify or facilitate the ministry among the North American Spanish-speaking world.

Challenges
The growth and development of the Hispanic church is confronted with a series of challenges related to the integration of Hispanics into an Anglo denomination.

Language
For the majority of the members English is a second language and therefore there are some who speak it poorly or, in some cases, little at all. There are persons who have lived in the United States for thirty years and still cannot communicate well in English. Although it seems impossible, this happens easily in the Hispanic colonies in cities such as New York, Chicago, and Brownsville, where the need to use English in daily living is minimal.

This struggle with the language gives the Hispanic a marginal place in the life of a church whose principal vehicle of communication is English. In addition, many times interpersonal relationships in the brotherhood are affected by the language barrier, since many concepts are different in the two languages producing misunderstandings that can cause unnecessary conflicts.

Culture

The Hispanic culture has certain basic characteristics that distinguish it from other ethnic groups: informality, subjectivity, and time flexibility, to mention only a few. A visitor to one of the Hispanic congregations will immediately notice that the worship is alive and informal without an established rigid pattern. When a Scripture is read in unison, it is possible that three or four different groups form with some finishing the reading five seconds after the leader. "Coritos" (choruses) with lively rhythms are preferred to solemn hymns sung in four part harmony. (Undoubtedly the classic hymn number 606 would lose something in the translation.) In addition, the preferred instruments that accompany the singing are not the traditional organ and piano but those of Indian, Spanish, and African origin: maracas, güiros, guitars, drums, and tamborines.

A panoramic look at the Hispanic culture reveals that it has a number of contrasts with the traditional Anglo culture. Shaking hands as a form of greeting is different in the two cultures. Hispanics practice it much more frequently and in church even young children can be seen using this form of greeting. To this we could add a hug between men and a kiss among women. These could be seen as sexually aggressive by someone who is not acquainted with the cultural background. The Hispanic stands out with his expression of affection, contrasting with the more calm and serene Anglo behavior.

It is interesting to observe a conversation between an Anglo and a Hispanic in which the Anglo continues to back away several inches while the Hispanic keeps moving closer until he has the Anglo cornered against the wall. This is simply due to the fact that one is more comfortable with several feet between himself and the other, while the other feels "the closer the better." This can easily produce misunderstandings: the Hispanic might feel the Anglo is impersonal and unfriendly; while the Anglo might interpret the actions of the Hispanic as overly aggressive.

The concept of time is different in both groups. In Spanish we say that the clock "no camina" (doesn't walk); while in English we say that the clock doesn't "run." This simple linguistic expression demonstrates the essence of both cultures toward the concept of time, since the Hispanic in general is very flexible in his daily schedule. This can produce tensions between the two groups. I will always remember the North American teacher who tried to teach punctuality to his Hispanic colleagues. He wanted to demonstrate that eight o'clock is eight o'clock and not 8:30, and to reach that objective he closed the doors so that those who arrived late could not enter. Undoubtedly this is an ethnocentric attitude that will produce negative repercussions.

There are other factors that could also be added to this cultural category: the concept of respect toward parents and other adults, family relationships, and stewardship.

Prejudice

Many stereotypes have been formed about Hispanics: "Hispanics are lazy, irresponsible, stupid, always late." This puts a stamp on persons with a Hispanic last name, no matter who they are or the background from which they come. I feel that this is produced by ignorance and narrow-mindedness. I will always remember vividly the meeting in which an individual, speaking about the Hispanic Ministries Department, asked why we now used the name "Hispanics" when before we were always called "Mexicans."

One interesting form of prejudice which has been experienced is that of some individuals who after serving in Latin America in some capacity with the Mennonite Church return as "experts" on Hispanic affairs. They try to analyze all situations in terms of the place and time in which they lived there without considering the marked differences that exist among the idiosyncrasies of the Hispanic American people.

Education

In my experience at Goshen College I have noted that those who study at the Mennonite colleges obtain not only a degree, but also a commitment to the Mennonite Church. Undoubtedly the formal education of Hispanics in the denomination's educational institutions will facilitate the Hispanic Anglo Mennonite integration.

Of course other secondary factors that hinder integration could be mentioned: the social position, the economy, imposed foreign styles and structures, and ignorance of the Hispanic historical and conceptual idiosyncrasies.

It is obvious that the Hispanic Mennonite Church not only has problems integrating with the Anglo Mennonite Church but also has internal problems. Truly the church has problems analogous to those of other Mennonite nuclei in Latin America, but to these must be added the many that are inherited from the social cultural situation in which the Hispanic in North America lives.

The Lack of Trained Leadership

A large majority of the Hispanic pastors have left the factory assembly line, the fields, and other humble tasks in order to minister. Without formal education they have stepped into the pulpit and have done the best they could. But now with the increasing level of education of their younger members, they feel threatened because "some of them have more education and theological studies than I." Thus begins the friction between the generations with the educated youth not returning because "the sermons are just spiritual milk" and the need is felt for solid substantial nourishment.

But the dilemma does not end here since the majority of those who have studied have received their training in Pentecostal or interdenominational schools. Thus the churches lack leadership with an authentic Anabaptist-Mennonite understanding and a clear vision of the organizational structure of the Mennonite Church.

The Generation Gap

As is natural in all transculturization processes, a gap develops between generations. It is natural that the Hispanic Mennonite children born and raised in North America will speak English, think English, and adopt North American ways. They will prefer to speak English since they do not feel comfortable with the vernacular of their parents. They may understand it but do not speak, read, or write it. Current reality presents gatherings with church friends where the parents speak only Spanish while the youth in an adjacent room speak English.

This will produce, and is already producing, a serious problem for the future church. Will there always be a Hispanic church of new arrivals and recent converts? Can we speak of second and third generations of Hispanic Mennonites? It will be, and already is, possible to identify second and third generations of Hispanic Mennonites but they will become members of Anglo congregations. This is proper because Mennonite Christians are being produced without regard to ethnic origin. But time will tell what this will mean for the maturity of the church.

Economic Dependence

The Hispanic conglomerate has a tremendous economic dependence on the Anglo church. There is a consciousness that this is not healthy, yet the question remains: when will self-dependence come? Presently the administrative committee is working with an ad hoc committee on a proposal for structural changes directed toward reaching this goal.

National Diversity

Although all speak Spanish and all are called Hispanics, there are basic cultural differences. These different historical cultural backgrounds can make the work harder and more difficult for pastors and leaders who attempt to bring all together under one roof with one name.

Take pacifism as an example. It will probably be easier to talk to a Puerto Rican or a Mexican American about nonviolence than to a Salvadoran, Guatemalan, or Nicaraguan who has seen his family members perish without mercy.

In spite of these internal and external inconveniences it has been possible to celebrate fifty years of a beautiful history. Many things have happened in those fifty years that have clarified both the weaknesses and the strengths, thus enabling the church to move toward the future with clear and precise goals. Without a doubt in the near future there should emerge some model Hispanic Mennonite congregations. These congregations will grow in number; they will be almost self-sufficient; they will contribute economic support for the programs of the Mennonite Church in general, both at the conference and national

Lawndale Mennonite
Church, Chicago,
Illinois.

Calvary Mennonite Church, Mathis, Texas.

Prince of Peace, Corpus Christi, Texas.

First Evangelical
Mennonite Church of
Brooklyn, New York.

Mennonite Church of the Lamb, Brownsville, Texas.

Pentecostal Mennonite Church, Woodburn, Oregon.

Bronx Spanish, Bronx, New York. Elton Avenue and 160th Street.

Church of the
Good Shepherd,
Goshen, Indiana.

level; they will create service programs for their communities; they will establish attractive programs for youth and young couples; and, therefore, thus will acquire a genuine commitment to the denomination.

It is obvious that the Hispanic Mennonite Church in North America has an endless number of significant challenges which it must face and attempt to resolve in order to better function, develop, and serve. But the light of the future is even more bright and promising when the glow of the past is remembered.

CONCLUSIONS

The first Mennonites that arrived in North America were not known for their evangelistic and missionary vision. However, interest in these two facets resurged in the nineteenth century as a result of the work of leaders such as John F. Funk and John S. Coffman. It was in this period, then, that activities were begun that were directly or indirectly fundamental factors in the development of the Hispanic Mennonite work in North America. Two activities produced by this missionary impetus, the Chicago Home Mission (1893) and the work in Argentina (1917), made important contributions to the establishment of the first Hispanic Mennonite congregation, Lawndale Mennonite Church (1932).

From this initial moment the church began to spread across the continent, but the church did not reach its major thrust until the sixties and especially the seventies, when it became organized, solidified, and self-identified. These advances have produced a phenomenal numeric growth that is worthy of praise. But all has not been rose-colored since the church has faced problems which it has attempted to resolve with the same faith and the same determination that have characterized it in the past.

It would be pleasing to attempt another evaluation and interpretation of the Hispanic Mennonite Church in North America during the centennial celebration. However, it is certain that it will not take that long to express the positive and significant changes that will have occurred in this important part of the Mennonite Church.

174

APPENDICES

APPENDIX A
EXTINCT CONGREGATIONS

Emmanuel, La Junta, Colorado

In August 1940, David Castillo, who had worked in Chicago during the beginning of the Hispanic Mennonite work, moved to La Junta for the purpose of working among the Hispanics of that city. Together with Fanny Boswell, a schoolteacher in the community, he developed a group which by 1963 was looking for a larger place in which to meet. The efforts of the group made it possible to purchase land for the construction of a church building which was dedicated in 1964 and carries the name, Emmanuel. Unfortunately the group, which now functions completely in English, is no longer related to the National Council.

Denver, Colorado

John Ventura, who was a member of the Lawndale Mennonite Church, moved to Denver in 1960. Ventura began to meet with a small group of Hispanics at the First Mennonite Church of Denver. Years later the group disappeared. Ruperto Guedea, who helped with this missionary work for several years, related the probable reasons for this disappearance: (1) the persons who attended were primarily older people, (2) the ministry was located in a limited area, and (3) the Anglo congregation provided no social contacts for the Hispanics.

La Capilla del Señor
(Chapel of the Lord)
Premont, Texas

In the early forties Amsa H. and Nona Kauffman moved from Tuleta to Premont, Texas. The Kauffmans, who were missionaries appointed by the

Mennonite Board of Missions, began to work in Benavides and Falfurrias, located near Premont. Since the work at Benavides did not prosper as they had hoped, they concentrated on the work in Premont and Falfurrias. The Mission Board purchased a small building in Falfurrias where the services were held. However, it was in Premont where the Kauffmans made good contacts with Hispanic families who offered their homes for worship services. With this encouraging reception a lot was purchased in Premont to which the small church building in Falfurrias was moved. Thus the Hispanics of Premont obtained their first church building.

The Kauffmans left Texas in 1946 and the small building was sold to the Southern District of the Mennonite Brethren, who already had several missions in the Río Grande Valley. The work continued under the leadership of several brethren until H. T. Esau arrived in 1948. Esau, a Kansas native, served full time in the work and immediately the small church building began to overflow with people. Therefore, he purchased additional land, expanded the church building, and constructed a parsonage. Although the work continued to grow rapidly, Esau had to discontinue his work due to failing health and decided to sell the property to the Mennonite Board of Missions, who had originally started the work there.

With the work again in the hands of the Mennonite Church, Richard and Luella Fahndrich were appointed to continue the ministry. The Fahndriches arrived in Premont in August 1960. In September of that same year Silvestre V. Zapata arrived and began to help with the work by selling Bibles. Robert L. Reist and his family transferred their membership from La Gloria and labored diligently in the work. The Fahndriches, in contrast to their predecessors, placed a lot of emphasis on reaching youth and adults with the goal of developing a self-dependent congregation. Although the desired level of economic self-sufficiency was not reached, the small mission became a dynamic congregation. The distribution of responsibilities among the members helped to create this lovely expression of congregational spirit.

In 1963 the trio that had been giving leadership to the work was broken up: the Fahndriches resigned to accept a work in Mexico, and Zapata died. At this point Reist, accepting the call of the South Central Mennonite Conference, took charge of the work on an interim basis and provided leadership with the assistance of several young people.

In 1964 Lupe and Seferina De León, who had recently been married, accepted the pastorate for a year. De León, the first Hispanic pastor of the congregation, made good use of the talents of young people such as Jesús Navarro and Ted Chapa to evangelize the community. In the summer of 1965 the De Leóns left for Hesston College for better academic preparation. Again the congregation was left without a pastor and Reist returned to assume leadership, again, with the assistance of a group of youth.

It was not until 1966 that they obtained a couple to put their hand to the plow: Keith and Rhoda Schrag. The Schrags knew Spanish so their work was simplified enormously. Their fluency in Spanish was a tremendous help in their communication with Hispanics who suffered loss due to hurricane Beulah which hit that region of Texas in 1967. These esteemed workers terminated their services in September 1968 and the lay leaders again assumed the responsibilities of leadership.

In June 1969, they obtained the pastoral leadership of Howard and Anna Beth Birky. During the leadership of the Birkys, who were acquainted with the work from their time in Voluntary Service in Mathis, the congregation began to show signs of new life: a new church council was formed, the youth were reorganized, community activities for children and youth were begun, women began to assume a dynamic role in the development of the work (a woman was named to the church council), and there was increased emphasis on Bible study and prayer meetings. But in 1972, the Reists, who had been bastions of the work for twelve years, decided to return to the United Mennonite Church of Premont and the Birkys, during whose four years of leadership the work had experienced a tremendous revitalization, left south Texas.

It was not until 1974 that they obtained Guillermo Tijerina as pastor of the Capilla del Señor. At that moment the congregation was passing through a time of very low membership due to the fact that many of the members had left the community in search of a better life, employment, and higher education. Young people such as Jesús Navarro, who obtained his degree in public administration and is employed as the director of the Department of Welfare in San Antonio, Texas, and Teodoro Chapa, who owns a restaurant in the same city, and families such as the Treviños, who now reside in Houston, Texas, where they joined the English-speaking Mennonite church, are examples of this tendency. At the present time the population of Premont is rapidly diminishing and the majority of those who have stayed are retirees. Unfortunately, due to this situation, the work was closed in May 1977.

Milwaukee Mennonite Church
Milwaukee, Wisconsin

Mario Bustos, a member of the Lawndale Mennonite Church, and Mario Snyder, the pastor, began to visit Milwaukee in May 1958, drawn by the desire to minister to the many Hispanics living in the southeastern part of the city. The majority of this area was populated by Puerto Ricans, Mexicans, and some Cubans. They obtained the facilities of the Summerfield Methodist Church and on June 22 they began to hold morning services. Visitation was carried out before and after the newly organized services. Also during the week they held Bible studies in homes.

In 1961 the group moved to the south side of the city, to a store at the intersection of Eighth and National Avenues. On July 4 of that year Bustos was installed as pastor in a service led by J. D. Hartzler. In 1963 the congregation had to vacate its facilities due to the construction of an expressway. After a prolonged search they obtained permission to use the facilities of an abandoned church building in the community. Finally, in February 1964, with financial help from the Illinois Mennonite Conference, they purchased a house located at 1239 West Mineral Street. The white brick structure was remodeled by a group of men from the Freeport Mennonite Church and the Illinois Mennonite Conference, supervised by Wilbur Smucker of Tiskilwa, Illinois.

The first baptism in the congregation took place in the National Avenue building when seven persons publicly committed themselves as members of the congregation. Later, in 1964, another five persons were baptized and eight accepted by letter of transfer in the Mineral Street building. By this time the congregation had 20 members and a Sunday attendance of some 75.

In 1971, Bustos left to accept the pastorate of El Buen Pastor congregation, at that time located in New Paris, Indiana. Thus the congregation was left without a pastor for two years until Elvin Snyder arrived in October 1973. Snyder had a broad background in Hispanic mission work; he had served for many years in Argentina, Puerto Rico, and south Texas. However, in this era the attendance of Hispanics began to decrease.

Snyder, already at retirement age, left Milwaukee in June 1976, and moved to Elkhart, Indiana. Snyder was followed by Joel Ortiz and Roy Jiménez, young leaders who, encouraged by the Hispanic congregations of Chicago, attempted to keep the work going. Finally, the work was closed on October 30, 1977.

Today there is a small group of Mennonites which meets on Sundays in a suburban YMCA.

Iglesia Menonita Evangélica
(Mennonite Evangelical Church)
Chicago, Illinois

In the early seventies, as we have related in chapter 4, the leadership of the Mennonite Community Chapel invited Victor Ovando to begin a work among the Hispanics of the community. The group prospered and moved to

APPENDIX B
CONGREGATIONS IN CHRONOLOGICAL ORDER OF FOUNDING

Illinois (1932)

Iglesia Menonita de Lawndale, Chicago (1934)
(Lawndale Mennonite Church)

Iglesia Menonita Evangélica, Chicago (1965)
(Mennonite Evangelical Church)

Iglesia Evangélica Menonita, Moline (1970)
(Evangelical Mennonite Church)

Iglesia Evangélica Menonita, 19th St., Chicago (1974)
(Evangelical Mennonite Church)

Iglesia Menonita Hispana, 51st St., Chicago (1977)
(Hispanic Mennonite Church)

Iglesia Menonita Cristiana, 50th St., Chicago (1981)
(Christian Mennonite Church)

Texas (1936)

Iglesia Menonita del Calvario, Mathis (1944)
(Calvary Mennonite Church)

Iglesia Menonita de Alice, Alice (1946)
(Alice Mennonite Church)

La Capilla del Señor, Premont (1960)
(The Chapel of the Lord)

182

Príncipe de Paz, Corpus Christi (1962)
  (Prince of Peace)
Iglesia Menonita Evangélica, Taft (1971)
  (Evangelical Mennonite Church)
Iglesia Menonita del Cordero, Brownsville (1972)
  (Mennonite Church of the Lamb)
Iglesia Menonita El Mesías, Robstown (1973)
  (Messiah Mennonite Church)

Ohio (1940)

Iglesia Menonita del Buen Pastor, Archbold (1940)
  (Good Shepherd Mennonite Church)
Primera Iglesia Menonita, Defiance (1957)
  (First Mennonite Church)
Primera Iglesia Menonita, Fremont (1980)
  (First Mennonite Church)

Pennsylvania (1950)

Iglesia Menonita Hispana, New Holland (1953)
  (Hispanic Mennonite Church)
Iglesia Menonita del Buen Pastor, Lancaster (1956)
  (Good Shepherd Mennonite Church)
Luz Verdadera, Reading (1960)
  (True Light)
Arca de Salvación, Philadelphia (1971)
  (Ark of Salvation)
Estrella de la Mañana, Pottstown (1974)
  (Morning Star)
Kennett Square, Kennett Square (1977)
Jesucristo es la Respuesta, Harrisburg (1980)
  (Jesus Christ Is the Answer)
West Chester, West Chester (1982)
Iglesia Menonita Hispana, York (1982)
  (Hispanic Mennonite Church)

New York (1957)

Primera Iglesia Evangélica Menonita, Brooklyn, New York

(First Mennonite Church) (1957)

Bronx Spanish, Bronx, New York (1964)

Templo El Peregrino, Manhattan, New York (1970)
    (Pilgrim Temple)

Iglesia Unida de Avivamiento, Brooklyn, New York (1974)
    (United Church of Revival)

Morris Heights, Bronx, New York (1977)

Efesios, Manhattan, New York (1977)
    (Ephesians)

Bethel Spanish, Amsterdam (1977)

El Tercer Cielo, Staten Island, New York (1978)
    (The Third Heaven)

Iglesia Cristiana Valle de Jesús, Brooklyn, New York
    (Valley of Jesus Christian Church) (1982)

Wisconsin (1958)

Iglesia Menonita de Milwaukee, Milwaukee (1959)
    (Milwaukee Mennonite Church)

Iowa (1963)

Segunda Iglesia Menonita, Davenport (1963)
    (Second Mennonite Church)

Iglesia Menonita de Muscatine, Muscatine (1969)
    (Muscatine Mennonite Church)

Oregon (1964)

Iglesia Menonita Pentecostés, Woodburn (1964)
    (Pentecostal Mennonite Church)

Iglesia Jerusalén, Salem (1977)
    (Jerusalem Church)

Iglesia Menonita del Calvario, Hubbard (1982)
    (Calvario Mennonite Church)

Indiana (1969)

Iglesia del Buen Pastor, Goshen (1970)
    (Church of the Good Shepherd)

Iglesia Menonita Emanuel, Marion (1977)

(Emmanuel Mennonite Church)

Idaho (1971)
Misión Cristiana, Caldwell (1978)
   (Christian Mission)

Arizona (1972)
Iglesia Menonita Emanuel, Surprise (1972)
   (Emmanuel Mennonite Church)

New Jersey (1972)
Faro Ardiente, Vineland (1973)
   (Shining Light)
Puerta de Sión, Trenton (1974)
   (Door of Zion)

Florida (1973)
La Puerta Hermosa, Immokalee (1974)
   (The Beautiful Door)
Voz de Salvación, Miami (1974)
   (Voice of Salvation)
Iglesia Seguidores de Cristo, Sarasota (1981)
   (Followers of Christ Church)
Ebenezer, Orlando (1982)

Washington, D.C. (1975)
Iglesia Evangélica Menonita Hispana (1975)
   (Hispanic Evangelical Mennonite Church)

Canada (1975)
Iglesia Evangélica, Edmonton, Alberta (1976)
   (Evangelical Church)
Iglesia Evangélica, Calgary, Alberta (1978)
   (Evangelical Church)

California (1978)
Monte Sinaí, Los Angeles (1979)
   (Mount Sinai)
House of the Lord Fellowship, La Puente (1980)

New Jerusalem Spanish Mennonite, North Hollywood (1980)

New Mexico (1979)
Iglesia Evangélica Menonita, Carlsbad (1979)
(Evangelical Mennonite Church)

Delaware (1981)
Centro de Amor Cristiano, Wilmington (1982)
(Center of Christian Love)

Michigan (1982)
Templo Menonita de la Hermosa, Kalamazoo (1982)
(Beautiful Mennonite Temple)

APPENDIX C
MEMBERSHIP 1960-81

STATE	CONGREGATION	CITY	60	61	62	63	64	65	66	67	68	69	70	71	72	73	74	75	76	77	78	79	80	81
Arizona	Iglesia Menonita Emanuel	Surprise	11	6	14	14	15	15	31	32	32	39	40	32	36	49	53	68	80	88				
California	Los Angeles																							
	Mennonite Fellowship	Los Angeles																					40	53
	Monte Sinai	Los Angeles																					12	37
	House of the Lord Fellowship	La Puente																						
	New Jerusalem	North Hollywood																11	11	14	20	19	21	25
	Spanish Mennonite	Hollywood																						25
Canadá	Iglesia Evangélica	Edmonton																						61
	Iglesia Evangélica	Calgary																						60
District of Columbia	Iglesia Evangélica Menonita Hispana	Washington																			12	20		15
Delaware	Centro de Amor Cristiano	Wilmington																						9
Florida	La Puerta Hermosa	Immokalee																23	22	16	21	28	28	24
	Voz de Salvación	Miami														12		9	28	10	10	17	16	13
	Iglesia Seguidores de Cristo	Sarasota									25	25	26					15						17
	Ebenezer	Orlando																						17
Iowa	Segunda Iglesia Menonita	Davenport						6	10	10											15	19	24	13
	Iglesia Menonita de	Muscatine																						
Idaho	Misión Cristiana	Caldwell																			30	29	30	38
Illinois	Iglesia Menonita de Lawndale	Chicago	62	62	58	60	60	52	55	62	62	61	64	78	78	78	80	80	74	81	92	89	89	94
	Iglesia Menonita Evangélica	Chicago												23	23	23	15	15	15	15				
	Iglesia Evangélica Menonita	Moline						22	22	23	23	23	23	35	42	46	30	30	35	37	37	42	42	42

187

STATE	CONGREGATION	CITY	60	61	62	63	64	65	66	67	68	69	70	71	72	73	74	75	76	77	78	79	80	81
	Iglesia Evangélica Menonita	Chicago Calle 19												37	37	37	35	19	36	50	45	45	19	45
	Iglesia Menonita Hispana	Chicago Calle 51																		15	15	15	16	37
	Iglesia Menonita Cristiana	Chicago Calle 50																					45	45
Indiana	Iglesia del Buen Pastor	Goshen													34	13	38	37	40	41	41	67	67	41
	Iglesia Menonita Emanuel	Marion																						9
Michigan	Templo Menonita de la Hermosa	Kalamazoo																						
New Jersey	Faro Ardiente	Vineland														27	21	29	24	24	25	29	40	66
	Puerta de Sión	Trenton																61	31	40	60	45	40	70
New México	Iglesia Evangélica Menonita	Carlsbad																						21
New York	Primera Iglesia Evangélica Menonita	Brooklyn	9	9	13	21	21	20	22	19	27	27	20	30	29	30	24	34	34	32	32	32	33	32
	Bronx Spanish	Bronx							10	10	12	13	16	18	18	18	18	18	18	16	16	17	16	16
	Templo El Peregrino	Manhattan												24	24	30	33	33	33	7	8	10	10	10
	Iglesia Unida de Avivamiento	Brooklyn														35	33	30	25	37	42	46	42	34
	El Tercer Cielo	Staten Island																			12	18	23	
	Morris Heights	Bronx																			24	20	20	17
	Efesios	Manhattan																			12	15	15	15
	Bethel Spanish	Amsterdam																			15	28	15	28
	Iglesia Cristiana Valle de Jesús	Brooklyn																						
Ohio	Iglesia Menonita del Buen Pastor	Archbold		13	13	13	14	13	17	23	31	31	30	31	30	30	38	38	38	38	38	46	49	39
	Primera Iglesia Menonita	Defiance							11	5	5	5	5	5	5		28	28	28	28	28	24	34	40
	Primera Iglesia Menonita	Fremont																						19

STATE	CONGREGATION	CITY	60	61	62	63	64	65	66	67	68	69	70	71	72	73	74	75	76	77	78	79	80	81
Oregón	Iglesia Menonita Pentecostés	Woodburn																					60	38
	Iglesia Jerusalén	Salem																			24	41	28	23
	Iglesia Menonita del Calvario	Hubbard																						29
Pennsylvania	Iglesia Menonita Hispana	New Holland	24	23	20	32	28	30	26	20	20	14	14	15	15	17	15	20	20	22	20	29	28	29
	Iglesia Menonita del Buen Pastor	Lancaster	19	19	47	41	44	22	27		2	7	19	22	27	62	60	90	59	36	38	46	26	46
	Luz Verdadera	Reading												15	18	29	33	36	54	54	60	72	65	73
	Arca de Salvación	Philadelphia																20	45	35	40	47	66	69
	Estrella de la Mañana	Pottstown																	14	30	41	48	37	38
	Kennett Square	Kennett Square																				12	10	18
	Jesucristo es la Respuesta	Harrisburg																						
	West Chester	West Chester																						
	Iglesia Menonita Hispana	York																						23
Texas	Iglesia Menonita del Calvario	Mathis	104	116	119	131	139	113	120	123	138	137	137	117	118	127	134	151	151	148	150	148	143	145
	Iglesia Menonita de Alice	Alice				19	19	24	23	25	28	28	27	28	28	28	28	28	28	28	35	36	25	40
	La Capilla del Señor	Premont	28	16		21	23	9	12	15	17	24	24	33	35	35	20	20	20					
	Príncipe de Paz	Corpus Christi		3		19	20	27	31	28	28	32	32	26	29	29	46	50	54	59	60	53	60	25
	Iglesia Menonita Evangélica	Taft															8	18	18	18	12	18	20	
	Iglesia Menonita del Cordero	Brownsville												6	13	13	50	59	59	59	60	59	100	98
	Iglesia Menonita El Mesías	Robstown													2	8			7	7	38	41	38	41
Wisconsin	Iglesia Menonita de Milwaukee	Milwaukee	7	13	17	17	17	24	22	22	22	22	21	21	12	21	13	13	15					
	TOTALES		277	261	320	369	400	377	439	417	472	488	498	604	661	803	861	1089	1122	1102	1216	1382	1532	1837

189

APPENDIX D

CONGREGATIONS BY CONFERENCES

Atlantic Coast Conference of the Mennonite Church
Bronx Spanish, Bronx, New York
Efesios (Ephesians), Manhattan, New York
Morris Heights, Bronx, NewYork
Primera Iglesia Evangélica Menonita, Brooklyn, New York
    (First Mennonite Church)
Templo El Peregrino, Manhattan, New York
    (Pilgrim Temple)

Franconia Mennonite Conference
Estrella de la Mañana, Pottstown, Pennsylvania
    (Morning Star)

Illinois Mennonite Conference
Iglesia Evangélica Menonita, 19th St., Chicago
    (Evangelical Mennonite Church)
Iglesia Menonita Cristiana, 50th St., Chicago
    (Christian Mennonite Church)
Iglesia Menonita de Lawndale, Chicago
    (Lawndale Mennonite Church)
Iglesia Menonita Hispana, 51st St., Chicago
    (Hispanic Mennonite Church)

Indiana-Michigan Mennonite Conference
Iglesia del Buen Pastor, Goshen, Indiana
    (Church of the Good Shepherd)

Iglesia Menonita Emanuel, Marion, Indiana
  (Emmanuel Mennonite Church)
Templo Menonita de la Hermosa, Kalamazoo, Michigan
  (Beautiful Mennonite Temple

Iowa-Nebraska Mennonite Conference
Iglesia Evangélica Menonita, Moline, Illinois
  (Evangelical Mennonite Church)
Iglesia Menonita de Muscatine, Muscatine, Iowa
  (Muscatine Mennonite Church)
Segunda Iglesia Menonita, Davenport, Iowa
  (Second Mennonite Church)

Lancaster Mennonite Conference
Arca de Salvación, Philadelphia, Pennsylvania
  (Ark of Salvation)
Bethel Spanish, Amsterdam, New York
Faro Ardiente, Vineland, New Jersey
  (Shining Light)
Iglesia Cristiana Valle de Jesús, Brooklyn, New York
  (Valley of Jesus Christian Church)
Iglesia Menonita del Buen Pastor, Lancaster, Pennsylvania
  (Good Shepherd Mennonite Church)
Iglesia Menonita Hispana, New Holland, Pennsylvania
  (Hispanic Mennonite Church)
Iglesia Unida de Avivamiento, Brooklyn, New York
  (United Church of Revival)
Jesucristo es la Respuesta, Harrisburg, Pennsylvania
  (Jesus Christ is the Answer)
Kennett Square, Kennett Square, Pennsylvania
Luz Verdadera, Reading, Pennsylvania
  (True Light)
Puerta de Sión, Trenton, New Jersey
  (Door of Zion)

Northwest Conference of the Mennonite Church
Iglesia Evangélica, Calgary, Alberta, Canada
  (Evangelical church)

Iglesia Evangélica, Edmonton, Alberta, Canada
    (Evangelical Church)

Ohio Conference of the Mennonite Church
Iglesia Menonita del Buen Pastor, Archbold
    (Good Shepherd Mennonite Church)
Primera Iglesia Menonita, Defiance
    (First Mennonite Church)
Primera Iglesia Menonita, Fremont
    (First Mennonite Church)

Pacific Coast Mennonite Conference
Iglesia Menonita Pentecostés, Woodburn, Oregón
    (Pentecostal Mennonite Church)
Iglesia Jerusalén, Salem, Oregón
    (Jerusalem Church)
Iglesia Menonita del Calvario, Hubbard, Oregón
    (Calvario Mennonite Church)

Rocky Mountain Mennonite Conference
Iglesia Evangélica Menonita, Carlsbad, New Mexico
    (Evangelical Mennonite Church)

South Central Mennonite Conference
Alice Mennonite Church, Alice, Texas
Iglesia Menonita del Calvario, Mathis, Texas
    (Calvary Mennonite Church)
Iglesia Menonita del Cordero, Brownsville, Texas
    (Mennonite Church of the Lamb)
Iglesia Menonita El Mesías, Robstown, Texas
    (Messiah Mennonite Church)
Iglesia Menonita Evangélica, Taft, Texas
    (Evangelical Mennonite Church)
Príncipe de Paz, Corpus Christi, Texas
    (Prince of Peace)

Southeast Mennonite Convention
Ebenezer, Orlando, Florida

Iglesia Seguidores de Cristo,Sarasota, Florida
(Followers of Christ Church)

La Puerta Hermosa, Immokalee, Florida
(The Beautiful Door)

Voz de Salvación, Miami, Florida
(Voice of Salvation)

Southwest Mennonite Conference

Iglesia Menonita Emanuel, Surprise, Arizona
(Emmanuel Mennonite Church)

Monte Sinaí, Los Angeles, California
(Mount Sinai)

House of the Lord Fellowship, La Puente, California

New Jerusalem Spanish Mennonite, North Hollywood, California

Virginia Mennonite Conference

Iglesia Evangélica Menonita Hispana, Washington, D.C.
(Hispanic Evangelical Mennonite Church)

APPENDIX E
LOCATION OF THE CONGREGATIONS

a building on Halstead Street, later to a place farther away at 2434 South Pulaski Street, and finally, to 2628 South Komenski Street. Unfortunately this congregation, that at one time had 23 members, reached a period of stagnation and in 1977 stopped receiving economic support from the denomination. Ovando continued his work independently.

El Tercer Cielo, Staten Island,
(The Third Heaven)
New York

This congregation, that began independently in August 1977, joined the Mennonite Church the following year. In 1980, the congregation that then had some 20 members, withdrew from the denomination.

APPENDIX F
THE MENNONITE BRETHREN CHURCH

The Hispanic work of the Mennonite Brethren Church has been centered in two states heavily populated by Hispanics: Texas and California. The work in Texas was begun in the late thirties. Missionaries Harry Neufeld, H. T. Esau, Ruben Wedel and H. F. Thomas played a significant part in its initial development. The denomination presently has 284 members participating in seven Texas congregations located in Edinburg (20 members), Garciasville (20), Grulla (50), La Joya (98), Mission (35), Phan (51), and Donna (10).

The work in California had its beginning in the decade of the fifties. Interest in reaching Hispanics began in the Reedley Mennonite Brethren Church in 1950. In that year a fund was established for missionary work among Hispanics, but unfortunately available workers could not be found. Therefore it was not until 1956 that the work really began when Dr. Arnold Schliechting, president of the Extension Committee, and other members of the Reedley congregation began to work in La Colonia, a small pre-dominantly Hispanic community located west of Parlier. This initiative has grown to 291 members in eight congregations: Dinuba (44 members), Fresno (23), Kingsburg (a new group with no official membership yet), Los Angeles (54), Orange Clove (25), Orosi (50), Parlier (51), and Reedley (44).

In summary, the Mennonite Brethren have a total of 575 members in 15 different Hispanic congregations. These congregations are located principally in small towns and minister primarily to Mexicans and Mexican-Americans.

The congregations in south Texas are organized into the Latin American Conference of the Mennonite Brethren and the Pacific Coast District.

The Mennonite Brethren Church now has a Hispanic leadership train-ing program located at the Mennonite Brethren Biblical Seminary at Fresno, California. The program offers courses in Spanish at the Bible Institute level and prepares the student for entering the regular seminary program.

APPENDIX G
THE GENERAL CONFERENCE MENNONITE CHURCH

At the present time the General Conference Mennonite Church has not developed a concrete program for the purpose of reaching Hispanics in North America. They have some 60 members in only three congregations, two of which began independently and then joined the General Conference Church. However, this does not mean that they do not have a history to tell and that they have not had a genuine interest in this minority, especially in the last five years.

Among the pioneers of the General Conference Hispanic work is the figure of Dr. Earl Stover, who, having lived in Puerto Rico for several years, was acquainted with the culture and language. He became interested in the Hispanic residents of Lansdale, Pennsylvania, around 1958. Victor Cardona was the first product of these personal contacts. This increased his interest and he asked Guillermo Chegwin to consider accepting the ministry to the Hispanic community. Chegwin accepted the challenge and beginning in March 1958 committed himself to visit the families weekday evenings and on weekends. The efforts of Stover and Chegwin resulted in the organization of a Hispanic department in the Grace Mennonite Church on June 29, 1958.

Today this congregation has a Sunday school attendance of between 40 and 50 and a membership of 29. The present pastor is Rafael Peralta (January 1982 to the present) who was preceded by Chegwin (1958-70), José Abreu, and José Rivera.

The second active congregation is located in Queens, New York, and answers to the name of Iglesia Cristiana Menonita Cuerpo de Cristo (Body of Christ Christian Mennonite Church). It began as an independent congrega-

196

tion when a group of persons, predominantely Colombians, met on January 29, 1979, in the apartment of Julio Dueñas to discuss the possibility of starting a Hispanic work. In the beginning they met in the apartment, later in the barbershop owned by the Dueñases, and finally in a church building previously occupied by the Plymouth Brethren, which can accommodate more than 100 people.

In conversation with Antonio Arévalo, who at that time pastored a Mennonite church in Bogotá, Colombia, Dueñas became interested in the Mennonites. Through this contact the congregation was visited by several administrators who worked in Hispanic affairs: Héctor Valencia in March 1980 and Ernst Harder in May of that same year. On May 5, 1981, the congregation requested membership in the Mennonite Church in a letter signed by its 24 members. It was officially accepted in April 1982, and Dueñas' ordination in August 1968 by another denomination was officially recognized in May.

As far as can be determined, this congregation has become well integrated into the denomination and promises to be a source of leaders.

In addition to the above-mentioned congregations there is a third one in Santa Fe Springs, 15 miles southeast of Los Angeles, California. This congregation, as did the one in New York, began as an independent group when in 1977 several persons began to meet after work in "John's Barbershop," whose owner, John Meléndrez, was the leader of the group. In 1978 the group was formally organized under the name, Whettier Masters House. The congregation, which meets in the Bethel Community Chapel, joined the denomination in March 1981, and in September of that same year Meléndrez was ordained pastor. The congregation now has 20 members and, although they are predominantely Mexican-American, holds its services totally in English.

There are two congregations that began in the late seventies as Hispanic departments in English congregations that today are no longer in existence. One is the group that met in the Calvary Mennonite Church in Liberal, Kansas, under the leadership of Manuel Vega; and the other is the group that met in the Houston Mennonite Church in Houston, Texas, under the leadership of the Víctor Alvarez family. In this case some 18 members remain and continue to meet with the English-speaking congregation.

In spite of these failed attempts and few nuclei remaining from these efforts beginning in 1958, the General Conference Mennonite Church has clear projections for the future development of Hispanic work in North America. In a summit meeting held January 31, 1978, it was mentioned that the General Conference has at least twenty congregations strategically located in places such as Chicago, Illinois; Wichita, Kansas; Denver, Colorado; Phoenix, Arizona; and Dallas, Texas. In Dallas there is a recently opened work under the leadership of Antonio Arévalo which provides assistance to Central American refugees. Meanwhile, in Minneapolis, Minnesota, are the seeds of a Hispanic congregation sponsored by Faith Mennonite Church under the leadership of Alberto Quintela.

The increased interest of the General Conference Mennonite Church in Hispanics was demonstrated again in the appointment of Ernst Harder as the first secretary of Hispanic Ministries. This position has as its agenda the determination of potential locations for ministry and the identification of willing and able leadership. On July 1, 1982, Alberto Quintela was appointed to that position.

Unquestionably the General Conference is quite conscious of the great challenge that the Hispanics of North America present, and in spite of its limitations, it is preparing to face the challenge of this large minority which in 1990, according to present studies, will exceed 27 million.

NOTES

Chapter 1

1. Menno Simons was born in Witmarsum, Friesland (in the Low Countries), he studied for the priesthood and was consecrated in 1524. One year after his ordination he had doubts about certain practices of the church: baptism, transubstanciation, violence, etc. On January 30, 1536, Menno Simons publicly renounced his relationship with the Roman Catholic Church, and soon afterward was baptized by Obbe Phillips, one of the pillars of Anabaptism. Menno wrote almost twenty books and pamphlets that were of great help for the Anabaptist brotherhood. At the time of his death, March 31, 1561, he was the recognized leader of the Anabaptist movement in the Low Countries and in Northern Germany. His influence was such that the Anabaptist movement of the Low Countries can be divided into three stages: before Menno, under Menno and after Menno.

For more detailed information about Menno Simons, see: H. S. Bender and John Horsh, *Menno Simons. His Life and Writings* (Scottdale, Pennsylvania: Herald Press, 1979).

2. For Mennonite history and doctrine, see: J. C. Wenger, *Compendio de Historia y Doctrina Menonita* (Scottdale, Pennsylvania: Herald Press, 1960); J. C. Wenger, *Mennonite Church in North America* (Scottdale, Pennsylvania: Herald Press, 1966); William R. Estep, *Revolucionarios del Siglo XVI* (El Paso, Texas: Casa Bautista de Publicaciones, 1975); J. C. Wenger, *How the Mennonites Began* (Scottdale, Pennsylvania: Herald Press, 1979); Kenneth Scott Latourette, *History of Christianity* (El Paso, Texas: Casa Bautista de Publicaciones, 1979), Volume II, pp. 136-38; Samuel Vila, *Origen e Historia de las Denominaciones Cristianas* (Barcelona: CLIE, 1981), p. 90; Cornelius J. Dyck, *An Introduction to Mennonite History* (Scottdale, Pennsylvania: Herald Press, 1981).

3. Argentina was the first Spanish-speaking country in which a Mennonite mission was established. The missionaries J. W. Shank and T. K. Hershey, together with their families, arrived in Argentina in September 1917. On Sunday, January 26, 1919, the first Mennonite worship in Spanish was held in Pehuajó. Today, the Argentine Mennonite Church has third-generation believers with a membership of more than 3,500.

4. The Mennonite missionary movement has been greatly extended throughout the Hispanic world. Today, in addition to Argentina, churches have been started in Colombia, Puerto Rico, Honduras, Uruguay, Mexico, Cuba, Bolivia, Costa Rica, Nicaragua, Paraguay, Panama, the Dominican Republic, Guatemala, Venezuela, Ecuador, and Chile.

Chapter 2

1. This was not the first Mennonite church in Chicago. In 1864 several Mennonites from Pennsylvania, who resided in Chicago because of business, organized a church and John F. Funk, also of Pennsylvania, served as its pastor.

2. Castillo was born in Mexico and became a Christian while living in Austin, Texas. In 1930, he came to Chicago in order to study navigation. Because of the Great Depression he had to change his plans: he abandoned his studies and began to work in a hotel. Before coming to Chicago, Castillo had worked very little with Protestants, but he came to Chicago with the zealous desire to tell others about Christ. He was a good speaker and soon after his arrival he began to preach occasionally in a Pentecostal Church.

3. The Hispanic Mennonite work begun in La Junta, Colorado, in 1923 was a temporary mission pastored by missionaries from South America during their furloughs. It was not until the arrival of David Castillo in 1940 that it officially became a church.

4. For this chapter we have used much from the following writings: Emma Oyer, *What God Hath Wrought* (Elkhart, Indiana: Mennonite Board of Missions and Charities, 1949); and J. Nelson Kraybill, "The Birth of the Chicago Mennonite Mexican Mission" (January 1978).

Chapter 3

1. Mennonite Central Committee, known as MCC, is a relief organization that is supported by almost all of the Mennonite groups and reaches around the world. Its central offices are located in Akron, Pennsylvania.

2. Home Missions, a division of the Mennonite Board of Missions, was established in 1955 with Nelson Kauffman as secretary. One of the primary tasks of the division was to try to expand the Hispanic work. Toward this end it began to take all those who were to work in Hispanic areas to San Antonio and south Texas to acquaint them with the community they were going to serve.

3. Program of the II Hispanic Mennonite Workers Retreat (June 23-26, 1975), p. 18.

4. Ibid.

5. Program of the II Hispanic Mennonite Workers Retreat (August 2-5 1977), p. 8.

6. Ibid., p. 19.

7. Program of the IV Convention of the National Council of Hispanic Mennonite Churches (August 14-18, 1978), p. 8.

8. Ibid., p. 20.

9. "V Convention of the Hispanic Churches," *Ecos Menonitas* (October 1980), pp. 4-5.

10. Ibid., p. 5.

11. De León, a native of Mathis, Texas, graduated from Hesston College and from Goshen College. In addition he has studied at the Associated Mennonite Biblical Seminaries in Elkhart, Indiana, and in several colleges and universities in Texas, California, Mexico, and Indiana. He has served on the boards of numerous national civic and ecclesiastical organizations. He was the president of the Executive Council of Latin American Broadcasters.

12. "Restructuring Continues," *Ecos Menonitas* (January 1982), p. 3.

13. Ortiz is a native of Coamo, Puerto Rico, and graduated from Hesston College, Goshen College, Eastern Baptist Theological Seminary, and McCormick Theological

Seminary, in Chicago, where he earned his D.Min. He has been a pastor for many years and has been involved in an endless number of projects of the Mennonite Church at the national and international level. His articles have appeared with regularity in the publications of the denomination.

14. "VI Convention of the Hispanic Mennonite Churches," *Ecos Menonitas* (October 1982), p. 13.

15. For the writing of this chapter we used the minutes of the Minority Ministries Council and the minutes of the administrative committee, Convention programs, articles from *Happenings, Ecos Menonitas, Gospel Herald,* and *Ahora,* together with informal conversations with Lupe De León, José M. Ortiz, and other leaders.

Chapter 4

1. Tobias K. Hershey was responsible for the thrust of the Hispanic work in two key states: Texas and Pennsylvania. Hershey served for almost thirty years as a missionary in Argentina and had worked in many other areas of the church. Hershey, who was born in Intercourse, Pennsylvania, in 1879, died in his seventies in 1956.

2. See Sanford and Orpha Eash, "The Hinojosas of Brownsville, Texas, *Gospel Herald* (July 15, 1980), pp. 554-55.

3. For a view of the Mennonite congregations in south Texas," see Paul Erb, *South Central Frontiers. A History of the South Central Mennonite Conference* (Scottdale, Pennsylvania: Herald Press, 1974), pp. 424-61.

4. See the Program of the Thirteenth Annual Assembly of the Council of Hispanic Mennonite Churches of Pennsylvania (April 30, 1983), p. 18.

5. Letter from Widmer to family and friends. 1958.

6. Quoted from Ronald Collins, "The History of the Bronx Spanish Mennonite Church. 1964-1971," December 3, 1973, p. 6.

7. Pastor Mateo, "Report from New York," in the program of the VI Convention of the National Council of Hispanic Mennonite Churches, p. 13.

8. "A Trilingual Church" (Interview with Mac and Mary Bustos, pastors of the Second Mennonite Church in Davenport, Iowa), *Ecos Menonitas* (April 1982), pp. 4-5.

9. For a panoramic view of the Hispanic Mennonite congregations in Illinois, see Willard Smith, "Illinois Hispanic American and Afro-American Mennonites: The New Urban Challenge" (Chapter 15), in *Mennonites in Illinois* (Scottdale, Pennsylvania: Herald Press, 1983), pp. 420-27. In addition, Smith includes in this section summary comments about the congregations in Milwaukee and Davenport, since they are related through the extension work of the Lawndale congregation.

10. This is the case with the Los Angeles Fellowship, a congregation that began in the fifties and today has a membership of 42. This congregation, which in the beginning was considered part of the National Council, has been separate since 1977.

Chapter 5

1. See "Immigration Training," *Ecos Menonitas* (April 1980), p.4.

2. "High-Aim Believes Program Philosophy," *High-Aim Highlights* (Spring 1981), p.3.

BIBLIOGRAPHY

Acosta, Elías. "Decisiones históricas 1974-1982" (Historic Decisions 1974-1982). Archives of the Hispanic Ministries Department, Goshen College.

"Adiestramiento de inmigración" (Immigration Training). *Ecos Menonitas*, April 1980, p.4.

Ahora (October 1975-June 1983). Archives of the Office of Latin Concerns, Elkhart, Indiana.

"Appoint Secretary for Spanish Ministries." *Mennonite Reporter*, June 11, 1979.

"Archbold, Ohio." *Ecos Menonitas*, April 1982, p. 8.

"Asociación Meno-Latina de Comunicadores" (Association of Hispanic-Mennonite Broadcasters). *Ecos Menonitas*, January, 1983, p. 8

Barahona, Rafael. Letter to the author about the congregations in Canada. January 1983.

Bell, Bonnie. "The Character of Lawndale Mennonite Church." April 13, 1978. Archives of the Hispanic Ministries Department, Goshen College.

Bender, Harold. *Menno Simons. Su vida y escritos (Menno Simons. His Life and Writings)*. Scottdale, Pennsylvania: Herald Press, 1979.

Blosser, Betsy. "The Lawndale Mennonite Church—a Brief History." December 16, 1976. Archives of the Hispanic Ministries Department, Goshen College.

Bolaños, Israel. Letter to the author about the work in Fremont, Ohio. February 1983.

Brochure of the Hispanic Ministries Department. Goshen College, 1979.

Brown, Al. Letter to the author about High-Aim. May 27, 1983.

Bustos, Mac. "Segunda Iglesia Evangélica Menonita" (Second Evangelical Mennonite Church). Historical Album 1982. Archives of the Mennonite Church, Goshen, Indiana.

Bustos, Mary "Corta historia de la Conferencia Hispana Femenil" (Short history of the Hispanic Women's Conference). *Ecos Menonitas*, April 1978, p. 11.

"Cambio de personal" (Personnel change). *Ecos Menonitas*, October 1982, p. 8.
"Carta de Carlsbad, Nuevo México" (Letter from Carlsbad, New Mexico). *Ecos Menonitas*, January 1982, p. 8.
Casas, Arnoldo. "Oficina de Literatura en Español" (Office of Literature in Spanish). Historical Album 1982. Archives of the Mennonite Church, Goshen, Indiana.
"Celebration and Transitions." *Gospel Herald*, March 15, 1983, pp. 184-85.
"The Chicago Mexican Mission," *Missionary Guide*, August 1951.
Collins, Ronald. "The History of the Bronx Spanish Mennonite Church (1964-1971)." December 3, 1973. Archives of the Hispanic Ministries Department, Goshen College.
"Concilio Hispano de Región V, Lancaster, PA." (Hispanic Council of Region V, Lancaster, PA.). *Ecos Menonitas*, April 1980, p. 9.
"IV Conferencia Femenil Hispana Menonita" (IV Hispanic Mennonite Women's Conference). April 1978. Archives of the Mennonite Church, Goshen, Indiana.
"VI Convención de Iglesias Menonitas Hispanas" (VI Convention of the Hispanic Mennonite Churches). *Ecos Menonitas*, October 1982, pp. 4-5, 13.
IV Convention of the National Council (Program). August 1978. Archives of the Mennonite Church, Goshen, Indiana.
V Convention of the National Council (Program). August 1980. Archives of the Mennonite Church, Goshen, Indiana.
VI Convention of the National Council (Program). August 1982. Archives of the Mennonite Church, Goshen, Indiana.
"V Convención Nacional de las Iglesias Hispanas" (V Convention of the Hispanic Churches). *Ecos Menonitas*, October 1980, pp. 4-5.
Cruz, Miguel Angel. "El primer graduado de Ministerios Hispanos" (The First Graduate of Hispanic Ministries). *Ecos Menonitas*, April, 1981, pp. 4, 12.

"Dallas, Texas." *Ecos Menonitas*, April 1983 p. 9.
"De la oficina de inmigración, Washington, D.C." (From the Immigration Office). *Ecos Menonitas*, October 1982, p. 10.
De León, Lupe. "Doce años de historia" (Twelve Years of History). *Ecos Menonitas*, July 1980, pp. 12-14.
_____ "Una iglesia con visión misionera" (A Church with Missionary Vision). *Ecos Menonitas*, June, 1975, pp. 7-8.

Directorio 1980-81, Concilio Nacional de Iglesias Menonitas Hispanas (Directory of the National Council of Hispanic Mennonite Churches 1980-81).

Directorio 1982-84. 50 Aniversario. Concilio Nacional de Iglesias Menonitas Hispanas (Fiftieth Anniversary Directory of the National Council of Hispanic Mennonite Churches 1980-81).

Dyck, Cornelius J. *An Introduction to Mennonite History*. Scottdale, Pennsylvania: Herald Press, 1981.

Eash, Sanford and Orpha. "The Hinojosas of Brownsville, Texas." *Gospel Herald*, July 15, 1980, pp. 554-55.

Encarnación, Ambrosio. "Iglesia Seguidores de Cristo" (Followers of Christ Church). Historical Album 1982. Archives of the Mennonite Church, Goshen, Indiana.

Erb, Paul. *South Central Frontiers. A History of the South Central Mennonite Conference*. Scottdale, Pennsylvania: Herald Press, 1974.

Espinoza, Guillermo. "Historia gráfica de la Iglesia Menonita Hispana (Calle 51)" (A Graphic History of the Hispanic Mennonite Church of 51st Street). Historic Album 1982. Archives of the Mennonite Church, Goshen, Indiana.

―――――――. "Un esbozo a la historia de la Iglesia Evangélica Menonita (Calle 19)" (A Sketch of the History of the Evangelical Mennonite Church of 19th Street). Historical Album 1982. Archives of the Mennonite Church, Goshen, Indiana.

Estep, William R. *Revolucionarios del siglo XVI. Historia de los anabautistas* (Revolutionaries of the XVI Century: A History of the Anabaptists). Buenos Aires: Casa Bautista de Publicaciones, 1975.

Falcón, Rafael. "Consulta de Currículo Anabautista en Cachipay, Colombia" (Anabaptist Curriculum Consultation, Cachipay, Colombia). *Ecos Menonitas*, January 1981, pp. 4-7.

―――――――. "I No Spik Inglis." *Festival Quarterly*, May-June 1980, p. 43.

―――――――. "La Iglesia Menolatina en Norte América: una interpretación" (The Hispanic Mennonite Church in North America: an Interpretation). *Ecos Menonitas*, April 1983, pp. 12-15.

―――――――. "La Iglesia Menolatina en Norte América: una interpretación" (The Hispanic Mennonite Church in North America: an Interpretation). *Ecos Menonitas*, July 1983, pp. 5-7, 14.

―――――――. Reports to the Coordinating Committee of Hispanic Ministries (1981-83). Archives of the Hispanic Ministries Department, Goshen College.

"Familias de nuestra iglesia" (Families of our Church). On the occasion of the 50th Anniversary of the National Council of the Hispanic Mennonite Church. August 1982.

Forjando nuestra historia. Ensayos con motivo del cincuenta aniversario (Forging Our History, Essays on the occasion of the 50th anniversary). National Council of Hispanic Mennonite Churches, August, 1982.

Gómez, Raymundo. Letter to the author about the Hispanic church in Carlsbad, New Mexico. January 1983.

Guedea, Ruperto. "The Mennonite Missionary Movement in the Americas. Initial Work in Chicago and Texas." April 12, 1983. Archives of the Hispanic Ministries Department, Goshen College.

——————————. Notes to the author about the work in Denver. May 1983.

Guete, Marco. "Iglesias Hispanas en la Conferencia General de E.U." (Hispanic Churches in the General Conference of the U.S.). Fall, 1982. Archives of the Hispanic Ministries Department, Goshen College.

Guía de Direcciones. Obra menonita en Latinoamérica, España y USA. 1978-79 (Address Guide. Mennonite work in Latin America, Spain, and the U.S. 1979-80). Aibonito, Puerto Rico: JELAM, 1979.

Happenings. Minority Ministries Council. February 1974.

Henry, R. E. Letter to the author about the Hispanic church in Caldwell, Idaho. January 1983.

Hernández, Donna. "Sigamos dándonos la mano/Let's Keep Shaking Hands." *Builder*, February 1979, pp. 17-23.

Hernández, Samuel. "Oeste de los Estados Unidos" (The Western United States). December 1980. Archives of the Hispanic Ministries Department, Goshen College.

Hershey, Lester T. Letter to the author about the Hispanic church of Washington, D.C. March 30, 1983.

Highlights. Spring 1981 and winter 1982.

"Hispanic Witness Begins in Kalamazoo." *Gospel Herald*, March 1983, p. 4.

Horst, Laurence. "Mennonite Community Chapel." *Gospel Herald*, May 24, 1960, p. 478.

Hostetler, John A. *Mennonite Life.* Scottdale, Pennsylvania: Herald Press, 1974.

Hostetler, Virginia A. "Hispanics Explore Maturity Theme." *Gospel Herald*, September 9, 1980, pp. 723-24.

"Iglesia hispana en Indiana instala un nuevo pastor" (Hispanic Church in Indiana Installs a New Pastor). *Ecos Menonitas*, April 1980, p.8.

"Iglesia Menonita del Calvario, Mathis, Texas" (Calvary Mennonite Church, Mathis, Texas). Historical Album 1982. Archives of the Mennonite Church, Goshen, Indiana.

Jiménez, Rodolfo and Elías Acosta. "Sandía en la historia" (Sandía in History). June 1982. Archives of the Hispanic Ministries Department, Goshen College.

"Junta de Educación aprueba programa de educación a latinos" (Board of Education approves education program for Hispanics). *Ecos Menonitas*, July 1979, p. 12.

"Kalamazoo, Michigan." *Ecos Menonitas*, April 1983, p. 8.

Kraybill, Nelson J. "The Birth of the Chicago Mennonite Mexican Mission." January 1978. Archives of the Mennonite Church, Goshen, Indiana.

"La Conferencia General da énfasis a la obra hispana en los Estados Unidos" (The General Conference emphasizes Hispanic work in the United States). *Ecos Menonitas*, July, 1978, p. 4.

"La Misión Menonita Latinoamericana en Washington, D.C. en acción" (The Latin American Mennonite Mission in Action in Washington, D.C.). *Ecos Menonitas*, November 1975, p. 6.

"La obra menonita hispana se extiende al oeste" (The Hispanic Mennonite Work Extends to the West). *Ecos Menonitas*, June 1975, p. 14.

"La reestructuración sigue" (Restructurization continues). *Ecos Menonitas*, January 1982, p. 3.

Latourette, Kenneth Scott. *Historia del cristianismo* (History of Christianity). Buenos Aires: Casa Bautista de Publicaciones, Vol. II, 1979.

Lauver, William G. "Resumen histórico de la obra menonita hispana en Pennsylvania" (A Historical Summary of the Hispanic Mennonite Work in Pennsylvania). Archives of the Hispanic Ministries Department, Goshen College.

López, Brígido. "Historia de las Iglesias 50 y 51 en Chicago" (A History of the 50th and 51st Street Churches in Chicago). May 17, 1983. Archives of the Hispanic Ministries Department, Goshen College.

"Los hermanos menonitas dan prioridad a los ministerios hispanos" (Mennonites Give Priority to Hispanic Ministries). *Ecos Menonitas*, April, 1981, p. 7.

"Lupe De León, Jr., nombrado Secretario de Misiones Domésticas" (Lupe De León, Jr., Named Secretary of Home Missions). *Ecos Menonitas*, January 1978, p. 7.

Martínez, Juan. Letter to the author about the Hispanic work in the Mennonite Brethren Church. March 15, 1983.

_____. "A Vision for Hispanic Ministries." *The Christian Leader*, April 26, 1983, pp. 40-41.

Mennonite Yearbook (1955-83). Scottdale, Pennsylvania: Mennonite Publishing House.

"Miami, Florida." *Ecos Menonitas*, January, 1980, p. 8.

"Minorities Goal, Brotherhood." *Gospel Herald,* November 13, 1973, p. 24.

Minority Ministries Council Minutes. Archives of the Hispanic Ministries Department, Goshen College.

Mojica, José. "Iglesia Menonita del Buen Pastor" (Good Shepherd Mennonite Church). Historical Album 1982. Archives of the Mennonite Church, Goshen, Indiana.

"Moline, Iowa." *Ecos Menonitas,* January 1980, p. 8.

Morales, Rose. "Cincuenta años en Chicago" (Fifty Years in Chicago). In the historical album of the Lawndale Mennonite Church. Archives of the Mennonite Church, Goshen, Indiana.

Muñoz, Héctor. "Reporte sobre la obra en Los Angeles, California" (Report on the work in Los Angeles, California). Archives of the Mennonite Church, Goshen, Indiana.

Muñoz, María Mercedes. Letter to the author about the Hispanic churches in California. December 1982.

"Muscatine, Iowa." *Ecos Menonitas,* January 1980, p. 8.

Neff, Charles. "A Short History of the Mennonite Home Mission in Chicago." 1935. Archives of the Mennonite Church, Goshen, Indiana.

"Nueva obra en Montreal, Canadá" (A New Work in Montreal, Canada). *Ecos Menonitas,* January 1983, p. 9.

"Nuevo Concilio de Iglesias Menonitas Hispanas, Lancaster, PA" (A New Council of Hispanic Mennonite Churches, Lancaster, PA). *Ecos Menonitas,* April, 1981, p. 4.

"Neuvo pastor en Chicago: Héctor Vázquez" (New Pastor in Chicago: Héctor Vázquez). *Ecos Menonitas,* January 1983, p. 9.

"Nuevos refuerzos para Milwaukee" (New Reenforcements for Milwaukee). *Ecos Menonitas,* March 1976, p. 11.

Núñez, Eliel. "Las Iglesias Hispanas de la Región IV de Indiana y Ohio" (The Hispanic Churches of Region IV in Indiana and Ohio). December 9, 1980. Archives of the Hispanic Ministries Department, Goshen College.

Ortiz, José M. "Church Growth Among Spanish-Speaking North Americans" in *Mission Focus. Current Issues.* Scottdale, Pa: Herald Press, 1980, pp. 442-52.

——————. "Oficina de Asuntos Latinos" (Office of Latin Concerns). Historical Album 1982. Archives of the Mennonite Church, Goshen, Indiana.

——————. "The Spirit of Ebenezer." *Mennonite Yearbook* 1982, pp. 9-10.

Oyer, Emma. "Home Missions Report." *Gospel Herald,* May 31, 1934, p. 180.

_____. "Relief at Chicago Home Mission." *Gospel Herald*, April 7, 1932, p. 29.

_____. *What God Hath Wrought*. Elkhart, Indiana: Mennonite Board of Missions and Charities, 1949.

"Pastorados" (Pastorates). *Ecos Menonitas*, April 1982, p. 8.

Pérez, Daniel. "Obra menonita en Florida y Washington, D.C." (Mennonite Work in Florida and Washington, D.C.). Fall 1980-81. Archives of the Hispanic Ministries Department, Goshen College.

Pérez, Irving. "Iglesia Evangélica Menonita La Puerta Hermosa" (The Beautiful Door Evangelical Mennonite Church). Historical Album 1982. Archives of the Mennonite Church, Goshen, Indiana.

Programs of the Assemblies of the Council of Hispanic Mennonite Churches of Pennsylvania (1971-83). Archives of the Hispanic Ministries Department, Goshen College.

"Raymundo y Clara Gómez y familia" (Raymundo and Clara Gómez and Family). *Ecos Menonitas*, April 1980, p. 8.

Reports and minutes of the Hispanic Ministries Committee of the General Conference. Archives of the Hispanic Ministries Department, Goshen College.

II Retiro de Obreros (Program of the II Worker's Retreat). June 1975, Archives of the Mennonite Church, Goshen, Indiana.

III Retiro de Obreros (Program of the III Worker's Retreat). August 1977, Archives of the Mennonite Church, Goshen, Indiana.

"Reunión de pastores hispanos de la Región II—enero 26-27" (Meeting of the Hispanic Pastors of Region II—January 26-27). *Ecos Menonitas*, April 1980, pp. 11-12.

"Robstown cambia el nombre de Misión Menonita" (Robstown Changes the Name of Mennonite Mission). *Ecos Menonitas*, July 1979, pp. 6-7.

Sandía Documents. Archives of the Mennonite Board of Missions, Elkhart, Indiana.

Santiago, Elizabeth. "La obra menonita en Pennsylvania" (The Mennonite Work in Pennsylvania). Fall of 1980. Archives of the Hispanic Ministries Department, Goshen College.

"Servicio de Inmigración—un centro de recursos para información sobre inmigración" (Immigration Service—a Resource Center for Immigration Information). *Ecos Menonitas*, October 1980, p. 7.

Shank, J. W. "Sixty Thousand Mexicans." *Gospel Herald*, December 1, 1932, p. 764.

Showalter, Louise. "La V Conferencia Femenil Hispana de iglesias menonitas" (V Hispanic Women's Conference of the Mennonite Church). *Ecos Menonitas*, July, 1980, pp. 3-4.

"Sinopsis histórica de la Primera Iglesia Evangélica Menonita de Brooklyn" (Historical Synopsis of the First Evangelical Mennonite Church of Brooklyn). Historical Album 1982. Archives of the Mennonite Church, Goshen, Indiana.

Smith, Willard H. *Mennonites in Illinois.* Scottdale, Pennsylvania: Herald Press, 1983.

"Spanish Church (Goshen, Indiana)." *The Gospel Evangel,* July-August, 1974, p. 5.

Stoltzfus, Dale. Letter to the author about the Hispanic churches of New York. June 28, 1983.

Suárez Vilela, Ernesto. *50 Aniversario de la Iglesia Evangélica Menonita Argentina (1919-1969).* Argentina: Comisión de Publicaciones de la Iglesia Menonita Argentina, 1969.

Tapes from the Sandía meeting. Archives of the Office of Latin Concerns, Elkhart, Indiana.

"Teófilo Ponce Family (New Paris Church)." *The Gospel Evangel,* January-February, 1971, p. 15.

Tijerina, Jacobo. "Breve historia de las Iglesias Menonitas del sur de Texas y Colorado" (A Brief History of the Mennonite Churches of South Texas and Colorado). Archives of the Hispanic Ministries Department, Goshen College.

Tijerina, María. "Conferencia Femenil 1982" (Women's Conference, 1982). *Ecos Menonitas,* July 1982, pp. 4-5.

"Una iglesia trilingue" (A Trilingual Church). *Ecos Menonitas,* April, 1982, pp. 4-5

Vallarta, Roy. "Milwaukee Mennonite Church." Archives of the Hispanic Ministries Department, Goshen College.

Vallejos, Jorge. "Iglesia Evangélica Menonita de Edmonton, Alberta, Canadá" (The Evangelical Mennonite Church of Edmonton, Alberta, Canada). Historical Album 1982. Archives of the Mennonite Church, Goshen, Indiana.

Vargas, Marlene. "The Lawndale Mennonite Church Celebrates 50 Year Anniversary." *Missionary Guide,* October 1982, pp. 1, 3.

Vázquez, Eva. "Las iglesias de Iowa." (The Iowa Churches). December 1980. Archives of the Hispanic Ministries Department, Goshen College.

Vázquez, Héctor. "Las iglesias de Chicago" (The Chicago Churches). December, 1980. Archives of the Hispanic Ministries Department, Goshen College.

Vila, Samuel. *Origen e historia de las denominaciones cristianas* (Origin and History of the Christian Denominations). Barcelona: CLIE, 1981.

"Washington, D.C." *Ecos Menonitas*, July 1981, p. 8.

Wenger, J. C. *Como Surgieron los Menonitas* (How the Mennonites Began). Scottdale, Pennsylvania: Herald Press, 1979.

——————. *Compendio de Historia y Doctrina Menonitas* (Summary of Mennonite History and Doctrine). Scottdale, Pennsylvania: Herald Press, 1960.

——————. *Que creen los menonitas* (What Mennonites Believe). Scottdale, Pennsylvania: Herald Press, 1979.

——————. *The Mennonite Church in America*. Scottdale, Pennsylvania: Herald Press, 1966.

Widmer, Gladys. "Iglesia Menonita del Bronx" (The Bronx Mennonite Church). Archives of the Hispanic Ministries Department, Goshen College.

——————. "La historia de la Iglesia Evangélica Menonita de Muscatine" (The History of the Muscatine Evangelical Mennonite Church). January 1983. Archives of the Hispanic Ministries Department, Goshen College.

——————. "La historia de los comienzos en las Quin-Cities de Iowa e Illinois" (The History of the Beginnings in the Quin-Cities of Iowa and Illinois). Archives of the Hispanic Ministries Department, Goshen College.

——————. "La Iglesia Menonita en Manhattan" (The Manhattan Mennonite Church). January 1983. Archives of the Hispanic Ministries Department, Goshen College.

——————. "La Primera Iglesia Evangélica Menonita de Brooklyn" (The First Evangelical Mennonite Church of Brooklyn). Archives of the Hispanic Ministries Department, Goshen College.

"Woodburn, Oregon." *Ecos Menonitas*, April, 1981, p. 8.

Yoder, Allan. Letter to the author about the Surprise, Arizona, church. January 1983.

——————. "Iglesia Menonita Emanuel" (Emmanuel Mennonite Church). Historical Album 1982. Archives of the Mennonite Church, Goshen, Indiana.

Yordy, Anna. "The Beginning of the Chicago Mennonite Mexican Mission." *Gospel Herald*, May 26, 1944, p. 146.

——————. "Home Mission Report." *Gospel Herald*, September 20, 1934, p. 536.

INDEX

213

Rafael Falcón, a native of Puerto Rico, is associate professor of Spanish language and literature at Goshen College, Goshen, Indiana. He also teaches Hispanic Mennonite History at that institution.

The author was the founding director of the Hispanic Ministries Department at Goshen College. He is presently the chairperson of the Commission of Congregational Education and Literature in Spanish and member of the Historical Committee of the Mennonite Church.

Falcó received his bachelor's degree from the Interamerican University of Puerto Rico and his master's and doctorate degrees from the University of Iowa.

He has published literary studies in various magazines in Mexico, Honduras, Spain, Peru, and the U.S., in addition to two books on the theme of immigration in Puerto Rican literature. He has also been a frequent contributor to Mennonite periodicals: *Ecos Menonitas, Alcance Menonita, Gospel Herald,* and *Story Friends,* among others.

Rafael and his wife, Christine, attend College Mennonite Church, Goshen, Indiana. They are the parents of two sons: Bryan Rafael and Brent Daniel.

❖❖❖

Ronald Collins is associate professor of Hispanic Ministries at Goshen College. He received his bachelor's degree from the University of Puerto Rico, a master's degree from the Associated Mennonite Biblical Seminaries, and the doctorate degree from McCormick Theological Seminary. Before teaching at Goshen he served as pastor for twelve years in Hispanic congregations in New York and Chicago.